T0311764

Cambridge Elements ☰

Elements in the Philosophy of Physics
edited by
James Owen Weatherall
University of California, Irvine

THE TEMPORAL ASYMMETRY OF CAUSATION

Alison Fernandes
Trinity College Dublin

CAMBRIDGE
UNIVERSITY PRESS

CAMBRIDGE
UNIVERSITY PRESS

Shaftesbury Road, Cambridge CB2 8EA, United Kingdom

One Liberty Plaza, 20th Floor, New York, NY 10006, USA

477 Williamstown Road, Port Melbourne, VIC 3207, Australia

314–321, 3rd Floor, Plot 3, Splendor Forum, Jasola District Centre, New Delhi – 110025, India

103 Penang Road, #05–06/07, Visioncrest Commercial, Singapore 238467

Cambridge University Press is part of Cambridge University Press & Assessment, a department of the University of Cambridge.

We share the University's mission to contribute to society through the pursuit of education, learning and research at the highest international levels of excellence.

www.cambridge.org
Information on this title: www.cambridge.org/9781108823852

DOI: 10.1017/9781108914765

First published 2023

A catalogue record for this publication is available from the British Library.

ISBN 978-1-108-82385-2 Paperback
ISSN 2632-413X (online)
ISSN 2632-4121 (print)

The Temporal Asymmetry of Causation

Elements in the Philosophy of Physics

DOI: 10.1017/9781108914765
First published online: May 2023

Alison Fernandes
Trinity College Dublin

Author for correspondence: Alison Fernandes, alison.fernandes@tcd.ie

Abstract: Causes always seem to come prior to their effects. What might explain this asymmetry? Causation's temporal asymmetry isn't due simply to a temporal asymmetry in the laws of nature – the laws are, by and large, temporally symmetric. Nor does the asymmetry appear due to an asymmetry in time itself. This Element examines recent empirical attempts to explain the temporal asymmetry of causation: statistical mechanical accounts, agency accounts, and fork asymmetry accounts. None of these accounts is yet complete and a full explanation of the temporal asymmetry of causation is likely to require contributions from all three programmes.

Keywords: causation, time, temporal asymmetry, statistical mechanics, agency

ISBNs: 9781108823852 (PB), 9781108914765 (OC)
ISSNs: 2632-413X (online), 2632-4121 (print)

Contents

1 Introduction

Our world abounds in phenomena that are 'temporally asymmetric', that is, directed differently towards the past and future. Bodies decay, but don't spontaneously rejuvenate. Smoke disperses in a room but doesn't naturally recoalesce. We remember the past but not the future. One of the most important and pervasive temporally asymmetric phenomena in our world is the temporal asymmetry of causation: the fact that (at least around here) causes always come prior in time to their effects. The causes of a gene mutation, a plane crash, or a failed dinner party only ever lie in the past of these events, never in their futures.

The temporal asymmetry of causation is so central to our thinking about the world that it is easy to take for granted. On reflection, one might take it to be a fundamental or primitive fact about how the world is – and so not something in need of further explanation. In Sections 1 and 2, we'll consider why there is a substantive empirical project underway to explain the temporal asymmetry of causation. In Sections 3–5, we'll then consider positive attempts to explain the temporal asymmetry of causation – including those using statistical mechanics (Section 3), features of agency (Section 4), and so-called fork asymmetry accounts (Section 5). While current explanations are incomplete, each programme provides resources for ultimately explaining why causes come before their effects.

Why, beyond curiosity, might we be interested in explaining the temporal asymmetry of causation? First, explaining its temporal asymmetry matters to understanding causation. A plausible constraint on any account of causation is that it can account for why causation is temporally asymmetric. As we'll see (Sections 1 and 2), not all accounts can, and some even conflict with the claim that causation is temporally asymmetric. Second, explaining the temporal asymmetry of causation in physical terms provides a model for how other temporal asymmetries might be explained, and sometimes provides a basis for explaining those asymmetries – including a record asymmetry (the fact that we have memories and other records of the past and not the future), an explanatory asymmetry (the fact that we typically explain events by reference to the past and not the future), and a deliberative asymmetry (the fact that we deliberate about what to do in the future but not the past). Insofar as understanding causation's temporal asymmetry helps us make sense of temporal asymmetries in general, we can also use resources from this programme to explain real and apparent features of time, particularly those that involve time being directed – such as the apparent flow of time and the apparent openness of the future and fixity of the past. Third, we learn lessons about the relation between fundamental physics, higher level sciences, and metaphysics through attempting to make sense of causation's temporal asymmetry. As we'll see, part of what motivates an empirical project of explaining the temporal asymmetry of causation is an apparent conflict between the relations used in fundamental physics and those used in higher level sciences – a conflict that is particularly sharp, given certain intuitive views about causation. By resolving this conflict, we have a broader story to tell about the unity of science, how philosophy helps us negotiate that unity, and the role of intuition in that negotiation.

1.1 What Is the Temporal Asymmetry of Causation?

To begin, we need some terminology. We will call *the direction of time* the direction in time from past to future. We will call *the direction of causation* the direction in time from cause to effect. To begin, to claim that there is a temporal asymmetry of causation in our world is to claim that, in our world, the direction of causation aligns everywhere with the direction of time – causal and temporal directions are globally aligned. If causation is temporally asymmetric in our world, causes always come before their effects and there are never any cases of causes coming after (or simultaneously with) any of their effects. We may need to revise this strict definition – I'll consider possible revisions in this section and the sections that follow. While I will sometimes talk of 'past', 'present', and 'future', these uses are always to be read as 'before', 'simultaneously with', and 'after' a particular time, respectively – such talk does not presuppose a so-called A-theory of time in which past, present, and future are different regions of time.

   The temporal asymmetry of causation is strictly stronger than three other asymmetries of causation. First, causation is *not* symmetric – **a** is the cause of **b** does not *imply* that **b** is the cause of **a** (unlike the sibling relation). Second, causation is *asymmetric* – **a** is the cause of **b** implies that **b** is *not* the cause of **a** (unlike the liking relation). Third, causation is *locally* temporally asymmetric – **a** is the cause of **b** implies that **a** comes before **b** in *some local* temporal ordering. The temporal asymmetry of causation implies these three asymmetries, but, in addition, claims a global alignment between causal and temporal directions – causes come before their effects in *all* temporal orderings.

   Most philosophers accept that causation is temporally asymmetric in our world. Some have defended the claim that there is *backwards causation* in our world in the context of quantum mechanics (Price, 1984, 1996: Ch. 8). We might also think we can change the significance of the past. However, these claims haven't gained widespread support. Moreover, even those who defend backwards causation in some settings still typically take causation to be temporally asymmetric when the causes and effects are large-scale 'macroscopic' events (Price, 1991, 1992a, 1992b). The temporal asymmetry of causation could be restricted to macroscopic causes and effects to allow for such views. However, for the most part, I will assume the standard view that there is no backwards causation in our world.

Some have suggested that causes often or sometimes occur *simultaneously* with their effects (Kant, [1781/1787] 1996: A203/B248; Carroll, 1994: 141–4). These proposals have also not received widespread support. Moreover, accepting simultaneous causation still leaves us with the problem of explaining why causes always come before their effects in cases that *aren't* simultaneous. Again, while we could restrict our investigation to non-simultaneous causation, I will assume the standard view that there is no simultaneous causation in our world.

1.2 What Might Explain the Temporal Asymmetry of Causation?

The temporal asymmetry of causation is robust and pervasive. It is taken for granted in much of our thinking about the world. For this reason, it may be tempting to think that causation's temporal asymmetry is a *necessary* feature of causation. Perhaps the fact that causes always come prior to their effects is *constitutive of* or *intrinsic to* the *nature* or *concept* of causation. If so, it might seem that the temporal asymmetry of causation warrants no further explanation. In the remainder of Section 1, I'll consider several proposals that treat causation's temporal asymmetry as necessary and not in need of empirical explanation. I'll argue that none of these proposals is successful and that the temporal asymmetry of causation is a contingent feature of our world – and so in need of empirical explanation.

One proposal takes the fact that causes always come before their effects to be part of the *definition* of the concept CAUSATION. The temporal asymmetry of causation therefore holds as a matter of conceptual necessity. Hume ([1739–40] 2000: Book I), for example, claims that the idea of causation derives in part from the idea of temporal priority.

However, even if the temporal asymmetry of causation is part of the *concept* CAUSATION, this fact merely shifts the explanatory burden. The question remains, why do we use the concept CAUSATION (in which causes always precede their effects) rather than the concept CAUSATION* (the same as CAUSATION, but in which causes don't always precede their effects)? One might argue that using CAUSATION rather than CAUSATION* is mere convention – in the same way that it is conventional to drive on the right in Sweden – and so is not in need of substantive explanation. However, because of the way causation is tied to our practices, the direction of causation doesn't appear to be merely a matter of convention (see Section 2.4). We explain effects using earlier causes (and not vice versa) and we decide on causes to ensure their later effects (and not vice versa). If the temporal asymmetry of causation were merely conventional, we would expect these practices to be temporally reversible without too much awkwardness – such as when Sweden switched from driving on the left to driving on the right. However, it doesn't seem that we could switch the temporal order of our practices of explanation and control with the same success. Put otherwise, if causation is temporally asymmetric by definition, we will be unable to explain why these practices are, non-definitionally, temporally asymmetric or why causal relations are apt to play these temporally asymmetric roles (Mellor, 1998: Ch. 10; Field, 2003; Price and Weslake, 2009).

A further argument against conventionalism is that we can make good *conceptual sense* of the possibility of backwards causation, that is, cases in which causes come before their effects (Dummett, 1964; Lewis, 1976). It is conceptually coherent, for example, that our rituals influence the past or that Dr Who using her time machine in the future *causes* her appearance in the past. If these cases are coherent, the temporal asymmetry of causation is not conceptually necessary. For related arguments against conventionalism, see Papineau (1985: 273–4), Mellor (1998: Ch. 10), Field (2003), and Price and Weslake (2009).

A second proposal for why we might not need to explain the temporal asymmetry of causation is that it is simply part of the *nature* of causation that causes always come before their effects – either as a primitive feature of causation or due to the way causation relates to laws. This proposal is compatible with views that take causation to be a primitive irreducible relation (Anscombe, 1975; Tooley, 1987; Carroll, 1994), views that take causal dispositions or powers as primitives (Greco and Groff, 2013), and views that take causal relations to be relations of nomic dependence (Kim, 1973; Armstrong, 2004) or otherwise closely related to laws. What ties these views together is the claim that there is a direction of time established independently of the direction of causation and to which causal direction must correspond. Mackie (1974: 225–6), for example, argues that the temporal asymmetry of causation is due to a temporal asymmetry in the laws of nature, which itself presupposes an asymmetry in time. Understanding the temporal asymmetry of causation might seem to require understanding the nature of *time's* directedness.

To defend this 'primitivist' proposal, one needs to explain why the direction of causation is necessarily aligned to the direction of time. One way to do so is to argue that causation, laws, and the direction of time all are related to *production*. Present states of the world, through time, causes, and laws, generate future states: 'what happens next flows from what is there already' (Mackie, 1974: 225). Laws (Maudlin, 2007: Ch. 4) or causal relations (Carroll, 1994) are the means by which the past produces the future.

However, this primitivist proposal is susceptible to a similar worry. If backwards causation or time travel are *metaphysically* possible (that is, possible given the nature of causation, laws, and time), then the nature of causation, laws, and time does not explain why causes come before their effects. The conceptual coherence of backwards causation and time travel may be enough to suggest that they are metaphysically possible. Results from physics provide further arguments. First, scientists and philosophers have entertained theories involving backwards causation as a genuine candidate for the physics of our world, including the Wheeler–Feynman theory of radiation, Feynman's theories of tachyons and positrons, and interpretations of quantum mechanics. Insofar as these theories are metaphysically coherent, the nature of causation, time, and laws does not explain the temporal asymmetry of causation (for discussions, see Earman, 1976; Horwich, 1987: Ch. 6; Friederich and Evans, 2019; Faye, 2021). Second, the equations of general relativity, that is, Einstein's field equations, have solutions that involve 'closed time-like curves'. These are possible trajectories such that objects travelling at velocities less than the speed of light could traverse these curves and find themselves previous in time to their starting point. The most famous of these solutions are from Gödel (1949). Assuming these features of general relativity remain in subsequent physics, backwards causation is compatible with the laws of our world and so is *physically* possible. If backwards causation is physically possible, this standardly implies that it is metaphysically (and conceptually) possible as well. For further discussions, see Horwich (1987: Ch. 7) and Arntzenius and Maudlin (2013).

A separate argument for rejecting the primitivist proposal is that, even if there is a primitive direction in time, this primitive direction needs to be manifest in physical phenomena if we are to be sensitive to it (Price, 1992a: 513, 2007: 264; Loewer, 2012: 132–6). We have no good model of how we could be sensitive to a direction of time that makes no difference to the kind of physical phenomena that we are sensitive to – such as the velocity and arrangement of matter. Even if there were a primitive direction, we would still need an account of whatever physical phenomena that primitive direction is manifest in and an explanation of why those phenomena are temporally asymmetric. Therefore, even accepting a primitive direction does not obviate the need for investigation into how various *physical* temporally asymmetric phenomena arise – which is precisely the project of those who reject a primitive direction of time.[1]

---

[1] A third argument against primitivism is that there is no direction of time independent of causal direction, as the causal theory of time suggests (see what follows in this section).

A third proposal for why the temporal asymmetry of causation is necessary is that the direction of causation *determines* or *defines* the direction of time – an implication of the causal theory of time (Kant, [1781/1787] (1996): A190–211/B233–256; Tooley, 1987: Ch. 9; Mellor, 1998: Chs. 10 and 11; Lowe, 2002: Ch. 18). If the direction of causation determines the direction of time, then it seems that causes must always come prior in time to their effects.

A first problem with this proposal is that the causal theory of time does not imply the temporal asymmetry of causation. Recall the fact that the temporal asymmetry of causation implies a global alignment between causal and temporal order. The causal theory of time only implies that the *local* direction of causation aligns with the *local* direction of time. The theory doesn't even imply that there is a *global* causal or temporal order. Compatible with a causal theory of time, there may be regions, even very large regions, where the directions of time and causation are counter to their directions in other regions. There may be causal and temporal loops.

One might respond by arguing that causal loops are metaphysically impossible or at least very rare. Lowe (2002: Ch. 18) argues that causal loops would violate conditions prohibiting circular explanation and so, at most, only small regions of backwards causation would be possible. Mellor (1998: Ch. 12) argues that causal loops would violate the logical independence of chances. These claims are countered by the arguments set out earlier in favour of the possibility of (widespread) backwards causation. If causal loops and backwards causation are possible, then explaining the temporal asymmetry of time using a causal theory of time will require explaining why, contingently, there are no causal loops or cases of backwards causation in our world.

A second problem with the causal theory of time proposal is that the causal theory of time does not explain why the direction of time and direction of causation go *this* way rather than *that* way, where *this* and *that* are defined by ostension or by reference to particular events. A causal theory of time does not explain, for example, why causal and temporal direction head away from the Big Bang and towards the direction in which the universe expands.

While the causal theory of time is plausible, it doesn't explain the temporal asymmetry of causation. For this reason, even those who accept something close to a causal theory of temporal *direction* and take the direction of causation (and other phenomena) to be the closest thing to what we mean by the direction of time (Reichenbach, 1956; Albert, 2000; Rovelli, 2018) don't take themselves to have explained the temporal asymmetry of causation. Indeed, their view about the origin of temporal direction only makes the business of explaining temporally asymmetric phenomena more pressing.

If we reject these proposals, explaining the temporal asymmetry of causation does not require us to look to the nature of time or the concept of causation – instead, it requires a, presumably empirical, investigation into how causation comes to be temporally directed at our world. The source of causation's temporal asymmetry will be not an asymmetry in time, but asymmetries in how phenomena are directed and arranged in time (Price, 1996: 16–21). Such an approach does not imply that causation is reducible – causation may be a primitive relation. Nor does it imply that we should disregard the nature of causation – we will still need some account of what causation is. However, such an approach does require that we investigate the conditions of the world, in broadly scientific terms, in order to explain how these conditions give rise to causal relations that are, contingently, temporally asymmetric.

However, perhaps you remain unconvinced. You might think that that there's an obvious fourth proposal that would explain causation's temporal asymmetry – a temporal asymmetry in the laws of nature. Such a view would not presuppose a primitive direction of time and so would avoid some of the arguments above.[2] The work of Section 2 is to argue against this proposal and use temporal features of laws and causation to show just how hard it is to fit causation into a physical view of the world.

2 Russell's Challenge

In *On the Notion of Cause*, Russell (1912–13: 1) argues for the wholesale elimination of causal concepts from philosophical vocabulary: 'The law of causality ... is a relic of a bygone age, surviving, like the monarchy, only because it is erroneously supposed to do no harm.' While most have disagreed with Russell's eliminativist conclusions, his arguments have led many to reject the idea that causal relations can be identified with the laws or law-like relations of fundamental physics.

Russell gives three main arguments for the elimination of the *relation* causation.[3] These arguments take the following general form:

1. Causal relations will be found in the relations of fundamental physics, if they are found anywhere.
2. The relations of fundamental physics lack features that are essential to causation.
3. Therefore, there are no causal relations.

---

[2] However, it would not avoid the argument of general relativity, which suggests that the laws of our world don't imply a temporal asymmetry of causation.

[3] Russell also gives other arguments, some of which are directed at the *concept* or *law* of causality.

While only Russell's third argument directly concerns causation's temporal asymmetry, all are relevant for whether causation should be identified with the laws or law-like relations of fundamental physics. However, while Russell takes the first two arguments more seriously, I'll argue that the third provides the strongest challenge for understanding how causation fits into a physical picture of the world. For further discussion of Russell's arguments and limited endorsements, see Earman (1976), van Fraassen (1993), Field (2003), Eagle (2007), Hitchcock (2007), Ladyman, Ross, and Spurrett (2007), Ross and Spurrett (2007), Farr and Reutlinger (2013), and Blanchard (2016). For more critical discussions, see Smith (2000), Ney (2009), and Frisch (2012, 2014).

2.1 Russell's First Argument

Russell's first argument for the elimination of causation is that advanced scientific theories don't mention 'causes' (Russell, 1912–13: 1): 'All philosophers, of every school, imagine that causation is one of the fundamental axioms or postulates of science, yet, oddly enough, in advanced sciences such as gravitational astronomy, the word "cause" never occurs.' These theories don't mention causal relations and don't identify particular events as causes and others as effects. Therefore, it might seem that there is no place for causation in an advanced scientific view of the world. Russell's argument can be formalised as follows:

P1. Causal relations will be mentioned in or identified by fundamental physical theories, if they exist.
P2. Fundamental physical theories don't mention or identify causal relations.
C. Therefore, there are no causal relations.

Let's look a little deeper into *why* theories of the advanced sciences that Russell has in mind, that is, fundamental physical theories, don't mention or identify causal relations. Imagine a closed system consisting of twenty-six billiard balls bouncing off one other. For simplicity, we'll ignore friction and electrodynamics; take the collisions to be elastic (without loss of kinetic energy) and take the system to be described by simple Newtonian laws of motion.[4] Say billiard ball A knocks into stationary billiard ball B, and then billiard ball B moves off. It seems that the movement of ball A *causes* the movement of ball B. However, the fundamental physical laws don't imply this. What the fundamental physical laws imply is that, given the positions and velocities of all twenty-six billiard balls at one time, t_1, their positions and velocities will be thus and so at another

---

[4] While Newtonian mechanics is strictly false, the argument holds for more realistic candidates for fundamental theories. I return to this point in Section 2.2.

time, t_2. The laws relate states of affairs of the *whole system* at different times – global states. The laws don't relate individual local states of affairs to one another and so do not select particular events as causes and others as effects. Therefore, when we ask a question such as, "What caused ball B to move off at velocity v at time t_2?", the theory provides no direct answer. The theory can tell us which of the balls collided with ball B, but this doesn't tell us what caused ball B's motion, without some further analysis.

Assume for the moment that Russell is right – theories of fundamental physics don't mention or directly identify causal relations. Why would this claim imply there is no causation? After all, there exist many things (for example daffodils, pain, and the colour blue) that aren't mentioned in or directly identified by fundamental physical theories. However, in the case of daffodils, pain, and the colour blue, no one *expects* to find them mentioned in fundamental physical theories. In the case of causation, a very natural assumption is that causation *is* fundamental to the operation of the world and is precisely the sort of thing that *should* be mentioned or directly identified by fundamental physical theories, if it exits at all. P1 is at least prima facie plausible.

In response, some have rejected P2 by arguing that scientists (even physicists) *do* use causal concepts (Suppes, 1970; Earman, 1976: 5; Smith, 2000; Hitchcock, 2007; Ney, 2009; Frisch, 2012, 2014). However, while scientists certainly use causal reasoning in the practice of science, such as giving explanations, applying physical theories, interpreting equations, and justifying dismissing certain solutions to equations (Woodward, 2007: 69), it's unclear why the necessity of causal *reasoning* or *representing* in science and uses of the word 'cause' in these contexts shows that causation is part of the *content* of scientific theories or that scientific theories directly identify causal relations. Nor is the use of causal concepts in 'higher level sciences', including much of physics, relevant to Russell's argument, which concerns *fundamental* physics – the (as yet undiscovered) scientific theory that is universal in scope and can explain the success of other sciences.

A second response is to reject P1 by arguing that fundamental physical theories *presuppose* causation, even if they don't mention it. Perhaps the physical laws must have a causal force 'backing' them in order to direct how a system evolves over time. Russell's second and third arguments provide reasons to reject this suggestion – whatever 'backing force' that physical laws require, it lacks features that we take to be essential to causation.

A third response, and the one I recommend, is to reject P1 and Russell's eliminativist conclusion by giving up the assumption that causation is fundamental to the operation of the world. If causation is macroscopic, emergent, or reducible, it is not something that we *would* expect to find mentioned in fundamental physical theories – so its absence shouldn't motivate eliminativism. Russell's first argument can thereby be accommodated by revising a natural assumption about causation. While removing causation from the workings of fundamental physics may be a surprising move, Russell's first argument provides no *additional* challenge for making sense of the place of causation in a physical view of the world. A fourth response is to reject P2 by arguing that causation is closely related to the laws of fundamental physics. We'll examine this response in Section 2.2.

2.2 Russell's Second Argument

Russell's second argument relates to his earlier observations about the laws of fundamental physics. Russell argues that that there is a conflict between satisfying three requirements on causation:

R1. Causes necessitate their effects.
R2. Causal relations are general (relating events of repeatable kinds).
R3. Causes and effects are separated by some time interval.

In defence of R1, causation, as it is commonly understood, seems to involve a *necessary* connection between two events (Russell, 1912–13: 2); once the cause occurs, the effect *has to* follow. In defence of R2, causation seems to involve a *general* relation between events – a relation that can hold of multiple particulars that we might actually observe (Russell, 1912–13: 7). While the causal relata might be particular events, they are events of a *type* that might plausibly be repeated, rather than events of a type that occur just once. Given that our universe is large and complex, this requirement suggests that causal relata are *local* events (or states), rather than global states of the universe. In defence of R3, Russell argues that there must be a separation in time between cause and effect (Russell, 1912–13: 5). Setting aside the possibility of simultaneous causation (the cause and effect overlap entirely in time; see Section 1.1), Russell argues that *contiguous* causation is not possible – the effect cannot follow *immediately* after the cause. Russell reasons that we can identify no 'last moment' before the effect begins that contains the cause. He also thinks that we should not allow for causes that exist for a time and then 'suddenly explode into the effect' (Russell, 1912–13: 5). Therefore, there will always be a time interval between the end of the cause and the start of the effect.[5]

---

[5] Russell's reasoning isn't convincing, but Russell turns out not to need R3.

Russell argues that these three requirements on causation cannot be jointly satisfied. To see why, let's consider the billiard balls again. It's tempting to say that, by the laws of Newtonian mechanics, if ball A moves in such and such a way at time t_1, on the way to a collision with stationary ball B, then ball B *has to* move off at velocity v at time t_2. However, this is not the case. It matters to ball B's subsequent motion that ball D is off to the side between times t_1 and t_2, failing to collide with ball A, and this is true for all of the other balls. Newtonian mechanics does not allow us to derive the motion of ball B without knowing information about *all* of the other balls at a given time, to ensure they won't 'interrupt' the collision of ball A with ball B in the time interval between t_1 and t_2 and prevent ball B from moving off. More generally and precisely, one cannot derive the state of *any part* of the system without knowing a linear combination of information about the positions and velocities of all other parts of the system or, alternatively, information about what is happening at each spatio-temporal point in the system. Local causes, of the kind that might be repeated several times, do not 'determine' or 'necessitate' their effects, given the kind of necessity we find in the laws of physics (Russell, 1912–13: 7–8). The upshot is that causal relations cannot be identified with the laws of fundamental physical theories.

One might worry that Russell's second argument depends on features that are peculiar to Newtonian mechanics or the metaphysics of lawhood. This is not the case. Consider, first, the fact that Newtonian mechanics takes global states as inputs. While there are candidate theories that take less than global states as inputs, none of them relates local states of the kind we would typically identify as causes and effects. The reason for this is that, as a quite general feature of our world, different parts of a single system can potentially interfere with relations between other parts. To correctly predict the behaviour of any system, one has to consider information about all of the potentially interfering parts.

When we look at the details of physics, there are further reasons for thinking that fundamental physical theories will not relate local states. There are toy theories that require information about less than the full global state to derive subsequent states, such as Newtonian mechanics with a restriction on faster-than-light 'influence'.[6] In this theory, information about each point in the backwards or forwards light-cone of a local state is enough to determine its state. However, this theory still does not identify individual causes. It takes as its input an ever-expanding slice of the world – a slice that increases in radius at the speed of light as the interval between cause and effect increases.

---

[6] This is a toy theory partly because general relativity doesn't involve a restriction on faster-than-light travel or influence (Maudlin, 2002: Ch. 3).

Furthermore, any theory that can reproduce the experimental results of Bell inequalities, predicted by quantum mechanics, must include correlations at space-like separations (separations that light cannot traverse). If these correlations are to be accounted for by a fundamental physical theory, the theory must require more than local information as its input. In fact, when we move from Newtonian mechanics to more plausible candidates for the fundamental physics of our world, the situation becomes worse. Quantum mechanics, in its various interpretations and variations, posits entangled states, implying that the full state of a system cannot even be *described* in terms of the states of its individual local parts.[7]

A second feature of Newtonian mechanics that might seem essential to Russell's argument is that the laws of Newtonian mechanics are *deterministic* – only one subsequent state of the universe is compatible with its current state and the laws.[8] However, determinism is not crucial to Russell's argument. Theories involving indeterministic laws, such as the Ghirardi–Rimini–Weber (GRW) interpretation of quantum mechanics, have the same global structure. The best that such theories can do in deriving subsequent states still requires information concerning every part of the system.

Russell's argument also doesn't depend on a particular metaphysics of laws or on the laws having *metaphysical* necessity of the kind Hume argued against (Hume, [1739–40] (2000): Book I, Part III). Russell's argument is compatible with 'Humean' accounts that deny that laws metaphysically necessitate, such as Lewis' 'best systems analysis' (Lewis, 1973b: 73–4). What Russell's argument relies on is the mismatch between the kind of necessity found in the laws and the kind of necessity found in causation, however deflationarily we characterise each of them.

The mismatch between local causal relations and fundamental physical laws is due to deep features of what we expect fundamental physical theories to *do*. What we ask of a fundamental physical theory is that, given full information about the state of the world at a single time, it delivers as much as can be known about the state of the world at a different time by the use of structural information about the world.[9] Put loosely, as much necessity as there is in the system should be reflected in the laws. How much knowledge the laws provide us will be limited by the kinds of patterns found in nature – there may be irreducibly indeterministic laws. However, a fundamental theory aims to allow us to derive as much as possible, given the limit to structural information. It is no surprise

---

[7] See Albert (1992), Maudlin (2019), and Barrett (2020).
[8] This is a rough characterisation of determinism – see Earman (1986).
[9] It is no easy task to say what counts as structural information.

that performing this task well (and without exception) requires global information as an input, rather than local events.

Having seen how much of a challenge Russell's second argument is, how might we respond? I'll begin by considering R3. I'll argue that, while R3 can be rejected, doing so won't help – Russell's argument depends only on R1 and R2. I'll then consider reasons to reject R1 and R2.

One might reject R3 (causes and effects are separated by some time interval) by claiming that causation propagates continuously through time, such that the cause and the effect occupy finite temporal intervals (one open, one closed). We might take causes to occur over a *closed* time interval contiguous with an *open* interval beginning the effect. This is one way to interpret the kind of propagation involved in process theories of causation (Dowe, 2000). Russell's arguments against this view (Russell, 1912–13: 5) rely on the claim that the real cause hasn't been identified, if the time interval of the cause that is enough to ensure that the effect hasn't been reduced as much as possible. Russell might be right that we would, intuitively, aim to reduce this time interval. However, in the case of laws, we do accept that earlier states can necessitate later states, even if we can't identify a 'last' finite moment at which the necessitating state occurs. A similar move should be acceptable for causation.

While Russell (1912–13: 7–8), Field (2003: 439), and Woodward (2007: 83) take R3 to be essential to Russell's argument, rejecting R3 does not resolve Russell's dilemma. Even if causes and effects are contiguous, an effect might still be interrupted by events or states other than the cause. In theories that allow for action at a distance, including Newtonian mechanics and Bohmian mechanics, events in spatially distant regions are relevant to the occurrence of the effect, even if they are temporally contiguous with the effect. In theories without action at a distance, all events spatio-temporally contiguous with an effect are relevant for its occurrence – so, unless we want to identify *the full set* of such events as causes (which R2 is meant to disallow), events that aren't causes are still relevant to the effect.

A better way to resolve Russell's dilemma is to reject R1 or R2. While rejecting R1 (causes necessitate their effects) by allowing for indeterministic laws doesn't help, there is another way to reject R1. One might accept that causes don't *by themselves* necessitate their effects, and instead claim that causes necessitate their effects given background conditions. The striking of the match is enough to necessitate its lighting, given that, for example, the match is suitably dry, there is sufficient oxygen in the room, etc. In what will turn out to be a similar move, one can also reject R2 and allow that causal relations can relate events that are not repeatable or likely to be repeated. Causal relations may then relate global (or very large) time slices of the universe – the striking of the match in just such a way, the exact constituents of the air, and so forth are, together, the cause of the match lighting. Rejecting R2 in this way requires a revision of what we typically mean by 'cause' – but it may be a palatable revision. By rejecting R1 or R2, we accept that relatively global slices are needed to necessitate local effects, given the laws – but we still take causal relations to be closely related to laws, either by identifying causal relations with laws (rejecting R2) or identifying causal relations with law-like regularities that hold given background conditions (rejecting R1).[10]

Arguably, either of these moves is a revision in how we think about causes. We talk of identifying 'the' cause, where 'the' cause is a local event – we don't typically identify global states as causes. We also, arguably, take causation to be a relation that holds directly between events, regardless of surrounding factors (Kim, 1973; Armstrong, 2004). However, causal locutions in philosophy and science have become sophisticated. We now speak of 'causally relevant factors', which include the multitude of events and background states that are relevant to whether the effect occurs – even if we don't typically identify them as 'the' cause. A standard view is that what we count as 'the' cause among causally relevant factors is simply a matter of pragmatics (Lewis, 1973a: 558–9).[11] Consistent with this standard view, we could take the global state to be a cause (rejecting R2) or any part of the global state to be a cause (rejecting R1) – leaving the business of specifying causes more closely to the pragmatics.

One might argue that either approach is still too permissive. Not all parts of a global state are causally relevant to a given outcome and so not all parts of global states can be (parts of) causes. The colour of Lizzy's hair is unlikely to be causally relevant to her successful pool shot, even if the colour is part of the previous global state. To gesture at a solution, the laws of physics may be able to demarcate sets of causally relevant factors – *pace* Eagle (2007: 160–1). In the example of the billiard balls, you don't need to know the *whole* state of the system at t_1 to work out what happens to billiard ball B at t_2. What you need to know is sufficient information about the system – information about what is happening at each spatio-temporal point or about each part of the system. The laws of physics tell us what aspects of ball C are relevant to ball B's subsequent movement – plausibly its shape but not its colour, since altering the colour won't imply a difference to ball B's motion, given the laws, but altering the shape may well. This is not yet a complete solution. Offering a complete solution will require a method for selecting appropriate contrast classes, such that changes in

---

[10] For options, see Smith (2000), Strevens (2007b), and Ney (2009). *Pace* Ney, it's not obvious that taking laws to relate parts of global states is incompatible with causation being about difference-making – see Glynn (2013) for discussion.

[11] See Schaffer (2016) for a summary of this debate.

the outcome given *any* of the contrast values implies causal relevance. In the case of the ball's colour, the appropriate contrast class would seem to be the full set of colours. None of these colours implies a change in the ball's motion, so the colour of the ball is causally irrelevant. However, selecting an appropriate contrast class will be difficult in other cases, particularly if the causal relata are concrete events or activities. For example, consider the case of Sam praying and a fire going out (Field, 2003: 439–40). Whether Sam's praying is causally relevant to the fire going out depends on what alternatives to Sam's praying we consider – do we consider contrast values where Sam is adding fuel to the fire or merely those where he is sitting quietly? If the former, Sam's praying is causally relevant. If the latter, it is not. However, while there are difficulties here, they are similar to those that arise within discussions of causation, namely over how specific the causal relata are, the selection of contrast classes, and the derivation of causal relations concerning actual events from regularities concerning event types.[12]

Russell (1912–13: 7), Hitchcock (2007: 48), and Woodward (2007: 84) argue that causal relations cannot hold between global slices – R2 cannot be rejected. Such a move would make the 'law of causality' (or the business of identifying causes) trivial, since any state A that preceded state B could be identified as the cause of B. However, while this response might work as an argument against the *law* of causality, our concern is with causal *relations*. Taking causal relations to relate global states would not make identifying causal *relations* trivial, in the same way that taking the laws to relate global events does not make identifying laws trivial. If one knows that global state F is followed by global state G, it may be trivial that F being followed by G is in accordance with the laws, but the science of identifying laws isn't trivial, since there are further restrictions on what the laws are. Russell himself suggests principles that undergird our practice of identifying laws (Russell, 1912–13: 15). Regardless of how exactly we explain the non-triviality of law-based science, the fact that events don't recur is not enough to show that there can't be a non-trivial exercise of identifying causes.

There are some challenges to these revisionist proposals. If we identify causal relations too closely with laws, it becomes unclear why we distinguish caus-ation from laws. If we think causation and laws have different roles to play (Section 2.4), they shouldn't be identified. However, putting aside these chal-lenges, Russell's second argument can be accommodated by relating causation

---

[12] There will be other difficulties as well, including pre-emption cases. However, again, the troubles are of a kind that arise when giving accounts of causation in general, even for those not motivated by Russell's concern. For an introduction to these issues and further references, see Fernandes (2018).

to the laws of fundamental physics either directly (if causation relates global states) or indirectly (if causation relates parts of global states, given background conditions). While these moves require some of our assumptions about causation to be given up, these costs may be affordable if they allow us to find a place for causation in a physical view of the world – and reject Russell's eliminativist conclusion. However, Russell has a third argument – an argument that identifies a crucial feature of causation that is not shared by the laws of fundamental physics: temporal asymmetry. While Russell doesn't give much weight to this argument, it is perhaps Russell's greatest challenge.[13]

2.3 Russell's Third Argument

Russell's third argument is that the temporal asymmetry of causation is in tension with the character of the laws of fundamental physics. In the laws of fundamental physics, 'the future "determines" the past in exactly the same sense in which the past "determines" the future' (Russell, 1912–13: 15). Because Russell has in mind deterministic laws, let's begin our discussion there. Examples of deterministic laws include the laws of Newtonian mechanics, general relativity, and the evolution of the quantum mechanical wave function described by the Schrödinger equation.[14] If the laws of fundamental physics are all deterministic, the state of a system at one time is enough to logically determine its state at *any* other time, given the laws. In this sense, laws are not temporally asymmetric in the way they determine events. If we take this logical determinacy as a guide to the way that the laws necessitate, any necessity in the laws operates equally well in both temporal directions. Therefore, it seems that causal relations can't inherit their temporal asymmetry from an asymmetry in how the laws determine or necessitate events. If one were looking to identify causal relations with laws or law-like regularities of fundamental physics, there seems to be a problem – causal relations have features that can't be recovered from the laws of physics.

Does Russell's argument apply if the laws are indeterministic? Arguably, it does if the laws take the same 'indeterministic character' in both temporal directions (Field, 2003: 437), such as by having similar well-defined stochastic probabilities in both temporal directions. Overall, if the laws are 'determinism symmetric' and determine events in similar ways towards the past and the future, it seems that causal relations cannot inherit their temporal asymmetry from the laws.

---

[13] Ney (2009) makes a similar point.

[14] In deterministic versions of quantum mechanics such as Everettianism and Bohmian mechanics, the evolution of the wave function is always in accord with the Schrödinger equation. However, this is not so for indeterministic versions such as GRW (see Albert (1992), Maudlin (2019) and Barrett (2020) for discussion).

Before evaluating Russell's argument, it needs to be distinguished from a different argument – one that relies on the claim that the laws are 'time-reversal symmetric' or 'time-reversal invariant', meaning that they take the same *form* in either direction or have no preferred 'orientation'.[15] If laws are time-reversal symmetric, the time-reversed sequence of a lawful evolution is also in accord with laws. Loosely, if one were to play a movie of the system evolving in reverse, its behaviour would still be in accord with the laws. Exactly how to formulate time-reversal invariance is controversial (Sklar, 1993: 246–8; Albert, 2000: 11–14; North, 2008), but typically the deterministic laws mentioned earlier are taken to be paradigms of time-reversal symmetric laws. While these laws are also deterministic, and so determinism symmetric, one can imagine toy examples of determinism-symmetric laws that are not time-reversal invariant (everything always moves towards the centre of the universe in one temporal direction). Russell's explicit claim is that the laws *determine* events equally towards the past and the future – not that they necessarily take the same *form* in both temporal directions. He is not arguing that the temporal asymmetry of causation can't be recovered from the *time-reversal symmetric* character of laws – he is arguing that it can't be recovered from their *determinism-symmetric* character.

Is determinism symmetry, without time-reversal symmetry, *sufficient* for Russell's argument? The answer depends on assumptions about causation. If causation is an as-yet-unspecified relation that might have various features, determinism symmetry is plausibly not enough to suggest that we can't identify causal relations with certain law-like regularities. Determinism-symmetric laws might be time-reversal *asymmetric* and the difference in the form they take towards the past and the future might directly account for the temporal asymmetry of causal relations. In our toy example, if causal relations are, by definition, law-like relations that lead objects to move towards the centre of the universe, then the temporal asymmetry of causation might reflect a temporal asymmetry in the laws. However, if causal relations are identified *merely* as the laws or law-like regularities of fundamental physics, then mere determinism symmetry is enough to raise the problem.

What if the laws are determinism asymmetric? If the laws are temporally *asymmetric* in how they determine events, there seems to be an easy response to Russell's argument. There are candidate theories of quantum mechanics that involve the collapse of the wave function, such as GRW, that imply that there are well-defined probabilities in the forwards temporal direction only. In response, first note that these theories are highly controversial, particularly as candidates

---

[15] For further discussion, see Farr and Reutlinger (2013). For arguments that appeal to the time-reversal invariance of laws, see Dieks (1986) and Norton (2009), with the latter discussed in Frisch (2014: Ch. 5).

for *fundamental* physical theories. Second, there are no good accounts of how a temporal asymmetry in the laws of GRW, for example, would scale up to a macroscopic temporal asymmetry of causation – particularly since quantum mechanics is required to recover much of Newtonian mechanics at ordinary length and energy scales. Similar arguments apply to other violations of time-reversal invariance, such as in neutral K-meson decay – *pace* Dowe (1992). These violations are too rare to explain the pervasive causal asymmetry we observe (see Maudlin (2007: 135–7) for discussion).

We might adopt one of the revisionist proposals above that identifies causal relations directly with law-like regularities of fundamental physics. In that case, any asymmetry in the laws may be enough to explain the temporal asymmetry of causation. However, if we reject revisionism and require that causation plays a different role from laws (Section 2.4), it's unclear how a temporal asymmetry in the laws of the kind being supposed could straightforwardly explain the temporal asymmetry of causation. Moreover, it should be borne in mind that this proposal assumes controversial physics.

Maudlin (2007: Chs. 4 and 5) argues that there may be a temporal asymmetry in the laws, even if the *equations* used to describe the laws are symmetric, and that this temporal asymmetry ultimately grounds the temporal asymmetry of causation. In other words, our laws may be determinism *asymmetric*, even if they are time-reversal invariant in their mathematical form. He further argues (Maudlin, 2007: 130–5; see also Frisch, 2014: 125, 133) that we need to appeal to an asymmetry in time, an asymmetry in which states *produce* which, to explain why we treat initial conditions so differently from final conditions – and that the temporal asymmetry of production (which Maudlin equates with the temporal asymmetry of causation) could therefore not derive from the distribution of matter in space and time.

While Maudlin's proposal avoids presupposing controversial physics, it presupposes controversial *metaphysics*. He posits a temporal asymmetry in the laws or causation that is independent of whether the laws can be formulated temporally symmetrically and independent of the initial macrostate of the universe. The explanation for the temporal asymmetry of causation goes *directly* from the metaphysical direction of the laws (or 'production') to the direction of causation, rather than going via how physical states are arranged in time. While one might accept metaphysical structure that goes beyond the structure countenanced by physics, it is surprising that metaphysical structure could directly explain the temporal asymmetry of causation without going via other physical states.[16] For

---

[16] For example, there is no guarantee that the direction of production will even be manifest in macroscopic temporal asymmetries.

related arguments, see Price (1992a: 513, 2007: 264), Price and Weslake (2009: 416–17), Loewer (2012: 133–6), and Farr and Reutlinger (2013).

Putting aside temporally asymmetric laws, there is a different response to Russell's third argument. This response is related to one considered earlier – a revision of our conception of causation to accommodate features of laws. In this case, we accept that causation is temporally *symmetric* and directed equally towards the past and the future (Ney, 2009). However, while the revision we considered above of allowing (parts of) global states to count as causes (Section 2.4) had *some* motivation in our regular practices of causal ascription, this new revision appears ad hoc – made merely to accommodate features of laws. Refinements in how we reason causally arising independently of Russell's arguments have led us to accept a much larger range of features as 'causally relevant' beyond 'the' cause. Therefore, there is some independent motivation for treating (relevant parts of) global states as causes. However, no refinements in how we reason causally, arising independently of Russell's arguments, have suggested that causation is temporally symmetric. The latter revision is motivated only by the fact that it would resolve Russell's challenge.

Moreover, to make this revision plausible, we would still want an account of why we *thought* causation was temporally asymmetric, why we apply causal concepts temporally asymmetrically, or why causation of the kind we're familiar with *is* temporally asymmetric (if we follow Ney in distinguishing two kinds of causation; see Russell, 1912–13: 20–1; Earman, 1976: 25; Farr and Reutlinger, 2013). If those explanations were given, whatever resources those explanations are based on would provide resources to potentially explain why causation *is* in fact temporally asymmetric. While explanations of the appearance of a phenomenon do not necessarily suffice to explain the phenomenon itself, in the case of causation, we have strong arguments that our causal concept picks out something significant for us (Section 2.4). Assuming that we're not massively mistaken about which relations are significant, there is a temporally asymmetric relation (typically called 'causation') whose temporal asymmetry is yet to be accounted for. While I have no objection to calling the temporally *symmetric* relation 'causation', the interesting puzzle is to explain why the relation that matters to us is temporally asymmetric, given that the laws are temporally symmetric. In this sense, taking causation to be temporally symmetric does not solve the hard problem of reconciling the asymmetry of causation with the symmetry of laws – at best, it gives the problem a different label.

Russell took his third argument to favour eliminativism about causation. However, insofar as eliminativism is the intended conclusion, there is an easy reply. Provided that we don't simply *identify* causation with the laws or law-like regularities of fundamental physics, there is no contradiction between accepting temporally symmetric laws and temporally asymmetric causation (Field, 2003: 438; Eagle, 2007: 158; Frisch, 2014: Ch. 5). Russell's argument instead provides a powerful challenge for making sense of causation's temporal asymmetry and for explaining the place of causation in a physical world. If the laws of physics lack the required temporal asymmetry, they can't be the basis on which to explain causation's temporal asymmetry. Therefore, even if causation is macroscopic, emergent, or reducible, we have no account of how its asymmetry arises.

2.4 The Role of Causation

So far I've argued that we should reject Russell's eliminativism and accept instead the empirical project of explaining why causation is temporally asymmetric. However, one might be tempted to make the reverse move and use Russell's eliminativism to evade the challenge of explaining the temporal asymmetry of causation. While one still might then need to explain why we *thought* causation was temporally asymmetric (Section 2.3), perhaps that project is, at least, less pressing.

Nancy Cartwright (1979) gives a trenchant response to this suggestion: doing away with causal relations in science and everyday life is not an option, because causal relations are needed to distinguish between effective and ineffective strategies. Say you're aiming to improve your fitness and notice that your fitter friends are wearing a lot of activewear. Should you adopt their clothing choice? Knowing there is a *correlation* between activewear and fitness will not help you decide. You need to know *causal* information about whether wearing activewear causes fitness (perhaps by motivating you to exercise) or whether they are *merely* correlated (such that the same causal factors that lead to fitness also lead to wearing activewear – perhaps an intention to exercise). Cartwright argues that a similar point holds regarding global laws. Global laws merely give us information about correlations, about what events are associated with one another, and so cannot play the role of distinguishing between effective and ineffective strategies.

Because Cartwright identifies a crucial role that causation must play, hers is a general argument against eliminativism. If she's right, causal relations are not mere stepping stones on the way to a more advanced exceptionless science, as suggested by Russell (1912–13: 8, 17–18). Instead, knowing about causal relations is needed for us to pick out significant parts of the global state that are effective strategies for achieving desired effects.

While much of the discussion focuses on effective strategies, a similar point can be made with regard to explanation (Cartwright, 1983: Ch. 4).[17] Scientific explanation is generally taken to involve citing factors *causally* relevant to the effect, not merely factors *correlated* with the effect – a distinction that the 'deductive nomological' model of explanation failed to capture (Bromberger, 1966). Insofar as we wish to give scientific explanations, it seems that we cannot do away with causation.[18]

Given the important role of causation in selecting effective strategies and explanations, and its absence from fundamental physics, there is a problem – what Hitchcock (2007: 58) calls the 'hard problem' and Field (2003: 443) calls the 'central problem' in the metaphysics of causation: how to reconcile the need for causation with its apparent absence from fundamental physics. The 'easy' (or at least more tractable) problem is to relate various causal relations to one another – work that interventionist and other accounts in the causal modelling tradition typically aim to do (Spirtes, Glymour, and Scheines, 1993; Pearl, 2000; Woodward, 2003). However, this 'easy' work will not answer the hard problem. Explaining the temporal asymmetry of causation, by contrast, plausibly will go some way to answering the hard problem. Temporal asymmetry is a core feature of causation that is (almost) entirely lacking from fundamental physical laws and that appears deeply tied to the roles of causation – effective strategies are future directed (we do things earlier to achieve things later) and so are explanations (earlier events explain later events). If we can make sense of how causation's temporal asymmetry arises, we will at least have the start of a reconciliation between Russell's and Cartwright's arguments.

Given causal relations feature in higher level sciences (and everyday life) but are absent from fundamental physics, a plausible assumption is that causation is primarily a *macroscopic* phenomenon – one that appears, most clearly, when we model systems using macroscopic variables (such as temperature, pressure, and volume) rather than microscopic variables (such as the position and velocity of all of the particles in the system). The explanations of the temporal asymmetry of causation that we'll consider all take causation to be primarily a macroscopic phenomenon, even if it may also apply at the micro level.[19]

---

[17] For discussion of the various roles of causation, see Strevens (2007a). For an argument that uses the explanatory role of causation to argue against treating the temporal asymmetry of causation as conventional, see Hausman (1982).

[18] One might wonder how we give explanations in fundamental physics if there are no causal relations. One option is to argue that there are causal relations in our *use* of fundamental physics (Frisch, 2014). Another is to argue that there are non-causal explanations in fundamental physics, which may or may not inherit the temporal asymmetry of causal explanation.

[19] A tempting view is that the extension of causal concepts to the micro level depends on the form that final fundamental physics takes – a live issue. See Ross and Spurrett (2007) for some of the ways that fundamental physics could be inhospitable to causal relations.

To answer the hard problem, however, it will not be enough to simply note that causal relations are *compatible* with the laws of fundamental physics. Fundamental physics, as I've defined it, aims to explain the success of higher level sciences. Since causal relations feature in higher level sciences, fundamental physics should at least be able to explain why causal relations are so useful (for prediction, explanation, and choosing effective strategies). If so, there will have to be some connection between the entities and relations directly mentioned by fundamental physical theories and causal relations. This is not to presuppose that causal relations *reduce* to the relations of fundamental physics – which may require further commitments regarding metaphysical reduction. However, at the very least, we need some way of deriving something about what higher level relations obtain using the resources of fundamental physics.

The accounts we'll consider all take causation to play a role and use a specification of what causal relations are or must do to pick out causal relations and explain their temporal asymmetry. These accounts don't typically aim to vindicate our intuitions about what causation is like or how its temporal asymmetry arises – partly because Russell's arguments are enough to question much of what we thought about causation. Because these accounts are to some degree interested in the *role* of causation, particularly for choosing effective strategies, they mostly fall under the banner of 'dependency' accounts of causation, which relate causation to probabilities and counterfactuals, rather than 'process' or 'physical' accounts, which relate causation more closely to physical production (for more on this distinction, see Ney (2009) and Schaffer (2016)). Effective strategies seem to be about effects *depending* on their causes – rather than the particular physical process that leads to the effect. Moreover, while effective strategies are clearly temporally asymmetric, it is less clear that physical processes are temporally asymmetric – perhaps explaining why there has generally been less interest in explaining the temporal asymmetry of causation using process accounts.[20]

The accounts we'll consider are as follows:

- *Statistical mechanical accounts.* These relate causation to counterfactuals and probabilities and use resources from statistical mechanics to explain the temporal asymmetry of causation (Section 3).

---

[20] Ney (2009) accepts process causation in both temporal directions. Dowe (2000: Ch. 8) defends a process account but uses a fork asymmetry approach similar to Reichenbach's (1956) to explain the temporal asymmetry of causation (see Section 5.2). For the argument that process accounts illicitly build in a temporal asymmetry of causation, see Dieks (1986).

- *Agency accounts*. These relate causation to the probabilities of relevance to deliberating agents and explain the temporal asymmetry of causation using features of agents (Section 4).
- *Fork asymmetry accounts*. These relate causation to patterns in probabilities concerning macro variables and use asymmetries in these patterns to explain the temporal asymmetry of causation (Section 5).

Our investigation will focus more on agency and statistical mechanical accounts, as recent work in these areas has been more focused on explaining temporal asymmetry. In Section 5, I summarise the state of these three programmes and consider their prospects for reconciliation.

As a final remark, since our focus is on explaining the temporal asymmetry of causation, I'll stay as neutral as possible on surrounding issues that are largely orthogonal – such as what the causal relata are (events, facts, states of affairs, values of variables, or something else) and whether causation fundamentally relates concrete particulars ('token causation') or abstract types ('type causation'). I will switch between different relata and types of causation as context demands.

3 Statistical Mechanical Accounts

Statistical mechanical accounts of causation derive causal relations from probabilities or counterfactuals. The relevant counterfactuals or probabilities are themselves evaluated using fundamental laws (among other things), so that causal relations inherit whatever determinacy they have from the laws. The challenge for these accounts is to explain features of causal relations that *don't* arise directly from the laws – including the temporal asymmetry of causation.

A key move in statistical mechanical accounts is to use resources from statistical mechanics to explain temporal features of causation. Statistical mechanics appeals to initial conditions to explain why systems exhibit temporally asymmetric behaviour, such as increasing in entropy towards the future, even if the dynamical laws are temporally symmetric. When applying this idea in the case of causation, statistical mechanical accounts use initial conditions of the universe to explain why causal relations are temporally asymmetric. While some are skeptical that there is anything *salient* about the initial conditions that could explain the temporal asymmetry of causation (Woodward, 2007: 103), those working in the statistical mechanical programme seek to identify such salient features. Because these accounts focus on identifying features other than laws that give rise to temporal asymmetries, they usually assume time-reversal invariant deterministic laws.

We'll begin with a brief look at Lewis' counterfactual account of causation (Sections 3.1 and 3.2). While Lewis' account is not a statistical mechanical account, statistical mechanical accounts draw their structure from Lewis' account, and inherit some of the same problems. We'll then consider Albert's and Loewer's statistical mechanical accounts (Sections 3.3–3.6). While Albert's and Loewer's accounts improve on Lewis' account, dealing with remaining problems has led statistical mechanical accounts to adopt features characteristic of agency accounts (Section 3.7).

3.1 Lewis' Counterfactual Account

Lewis (1973a, 1979) analyses causal relations using counterfactuals. Counterfactuals are typically expressed in English by subjunctive conditions of the form: 'if **a** *were* to happen, **b** *would* happen', where **a** is the *antecedent* and **b** is the *consequent*. According to Lewis, distinct particular events **a** and **b** are causally related if and only if **b** counterfactually depends on **a** or there is a chain of counterfactual dependencies relating them. **b** *counterfactually depends* on **a** if and only if the following two counterfactuals are true: 'if **a** were to happen, **b** would happen' and 'if **a** were not to happen, **b** would not happen'. 'If **a** were to happen, **b** would happen' is true if both **a** and **b** occur in the actual world. If they do, then, to see whether **b** counterfactually depends on **a**, we need only to determine whether or not the following is true: 'if **a** were *not* to happen, **b** would *not* happen'. These are the kinds of counterfactuals that we will typically be interested in evaluating.

Lewis gives a 'recipe' for evaluating such counterfactuals. The aim is that, if counterfactuals are evaluated using this recipe (in our world), they will imply the causal relations that we take to obtain. They will also be such that causes always come before their effects; therefore, the recipe can be used to explain the temporal asymmetry of causation. Because backwards causation requires some backwards counterfactual dependency, if earlier events never counterfactually depend on later (or simultaneous) events, causes will always come before their effects – and the temporal asymmetry of causation will be explained. The aim is to avoid putting in the temporal asymmetry 'by hand'. We don't evaluate counterfactuals using an explicitly temporally asymmetric method. Instead, we use a temporally neutral method that, combined with physically asymmetries in our world, delivers a temporal asymmetry of causation. By adopting this approach, the method aims to reveal the physical *source* of temporal asymmetries.

Lewis evaluates counterfactuals by considering 'nearby' counterfactual worlds.[21] To evaluate the statement 'if **a** were not to happen, **b** would not happen', given **a** and **b** occur in the actual world, we consider worlds that are very much like our world (they are 'nearby'), but where **a** does not happen.

---

[21] These worlds may be real (Lewis) or abstract constructions (Albert and Loewer).

If **b** does not happen in all the nearest counterfactual worlds, the counterfactual is true. The nearest worlds that are relevant for evaluating these counterfactuals have the same laws as the actual world, except for a small spatio-temporal area where the laws are different – known as a 'miracle'. Worlds are nearer to ours the fewer miracles they have. Of secondary importance, worlds are nearer to ours if they match the actual world in regard to particular matters of fact in as large a spatio-temporal area as possible (consistent with minimising miracles). There must be some compromise here, for, if there are to be any areas of perfect match, counterfactual worlds cannot have exactly the same laws as the actual world. Assuming deterministic laws, any difference in the counterfactual world at one time (required to satisfy the antecedent) will imply differences to the counterfactual world at *every* other time. To allow for times where the actual and counterfactual worlds match exactly, and so to rule out backwards counterfactual dependence, Lewis allows for miracles.

Lewis argues that, given the recipe above, the nearest counterfactual worlds to the actual world will have the following features. They will match the actual world perfectly in particular matters of fact until a short time before the antecedent. A 'miracle' then occurs that leads, via laws matching our own, to the satisfaction of the antecedent. After the antecedent, the laws determine the future states of the counterfactual world. Its future may be very different from ours. If the nearest worlds have these general features, events before the miracle will not counterfactually depend on the antecedent, since they remain unchanged in counterfactual worlds. Therefore, Lewis' account will have ruled out most forms of backwards counterfactual dependence.

Lewis' account only rules out backwards counterfactual dependence if nearby worlds have a perfect match *before* the antecedent (and so miracles before the antecedent), rather than a perfect match *after* the antecedent (and so miracles after the antecedent). Lewis (1979) argues that his recipe will deliver this result because our world has an asymmetry of 'traces' or 'overdetermination'. According to Lewis, traces are localised events that, given the laws, determine that an event occurs. Traces are events such as memories, recordings, and so forth. Lewis argues that, in our world, events leave many traces in their futures, but never in their pasts. An event such as Nixon pressing a button leaves traces such as Nixon's memory, a signal in the wire, light waves, and so forth. Each of these traces is taken to be enough, given the laws, to determine that Nixon pressed the button. By contrast, it seems that there aren't localised events previous to Nixon's pressing the button that are enough to determine that he does so – it takes a vast concordance of events to imply Nixon's button pressing.

If there is this asymmetry of traces, then it will take fewer miracles to satisfy a counterfactual antecedent by placing the miracles *before* the antecedent, rather

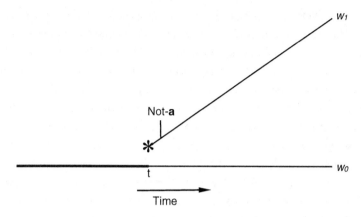

Figure 1 The actual world (w_0) compared with a nearby counterfactual world (w_1), given Lewis' recipe for evaluating counterfactuals. The worlds match perfectly before time t – when a small miracle (*) occurs – but are different after t.

than after. In Nixon's case, a few neurons firing differently *earlier* than the antecedent may be enough to imply Nixon does not press the button. However, it seems, placing miracles after the antecedent will mean that *all* the records of Nixon pressing the button will have to be removed using miracles, since each record is enough, given the laws, to determine the actual event. However, using many miracles is inconsistent with Lewis' recipe. Because miracles are placed before the antecedent, and not after, events before the miracle will remain unchanged in counterfactual worlds, while events after may be different (Figure 1). Therefore, the future counterfactually depends on the present, while the past does not.

3.2 Objections to Lewis' Account

Lewis' explanation faces three major objections. Two of these carry over to statistical mechanical accounts, while the third motivates statistical mechanical accounts. For further discussions of Lewis' account, see Bennett (1984), Horwich (1987: Ch. 10), Price (1996: Ch. 6), Hausman (1998: Ch. 6), Field (2003), and Price and Weslake (2009).

A first concern is that Lewis' account implies that there is backwards counterfactual dependence during the 'transition period' – the time between the miracle and the antecedent. Events during the transition period may counterfactually depend on the antecedent. Insofar as they do, it seems that this backwards counterfactual dependence will imply backwards causation – and Lewis won't have explained the temporal asymmetry of causation.

In response, Lewis (1979, 1981b) argues that, while there may be backwards counterfactual dependence during the transition period, it won't take any particular form. Because it is indeterminate precisely which miracle would have occurred, there aren't determinate facts about which events during the transition period depend on the antecedent. However, as Vihvelin (1991) and Field (2003) point out, it's hard to see why there must be determinate backwards counterfactual dependence regarding *particular* events for there to be a problem. It is certainly determinate that there will be *some* backwards counterfactual dependence. Furthermore, minimising the number of miracles may sometimes require very long transition periods (Bennett, 1984). One can also envisage systems where it will be determinate *when* the miracle occurs and the transition period is still long.

A second concern is that Lewis doesn't adequately justify why counterfactuals should be evaluated using his recipe (Bennett, 1984; Horwich, 1987: 172; Woodward, 2003: 137; Price and Weslake, 2009). Given the role of causation in choosing effective strategies (Section 2.4) and, perhaps, in rational decision-making (Lewis, 1981a; Eells, 1982: Ch. 4; Horwich, 1987: Ch. 11), it seems there should be some account of why causal relations derived from counterfactuals evaluated using Lewis' recipe are able to play these roles. Why, for example, does perfect match matter so much more than imperfect match? Why should we accept miracles? Lewis has little to say on these issues. When Lewis first introduces his recipe, he takes it to track our 'opinions about comparative similarity' (Lewis, 1973b: 95). Later, he is explicit that the recipe is reverse-engineered to deliver the intuitively right results (Lewis, 1979: 466–7). Lewis is explicit that his standards are tailored to rule out backwards counterfactual dependence (Lewis, 1986: 181–2). However, if the recipe is *engineered* to rule out backwards counterfactual dependence, it's not clear it can provide any deeper understanding into *why* causation is temporally asymmetric.

A third concern, the most serious, is that there is no asymmetry of overdetermination of the kind Lewis relies on. While events do leave 'records' in their futures, these records are not enough, individually or together, given the laws, to determine past events – they are not 'traces' in Lewis' sense. As we will see, because there is no asymmetry of traces, it turns out that Lewis' recipe can lead equally well to miracles being placed *after* the antecedent, implying large-scale backwards counterfactual dependence. Even before we consider more advanced versions of this objection (Elga, 2001), we can anticipate it by recalling Russell's second argument (Section 2.2; see also Arntzenius, 1990). Russell argues that nothing less than information concerning *every* part of a system determines whether an event at another time occurs, given the laws. An apparent 'trace' such as Nixon's memory is not enough to determine that Nixon presses the button.

One might think that, even if localised events are not enough to *determine* an event, perhaps they are enough to render it *probable*. If so, perhaps Lewis' account implies a probabilistic temporal asymmetry of counterfactual dependence. Elga (2001), following Earman (1976: 21) and Albert (1994), argues that even a probabilistic asymmetry is not implied. Considering why will provide the foundations for more successful statistical mechanical accounts.

Begin by distinguishing between a system's macrostate and microstate. The macrostate of a system is characterised by its macroscopic properties, such as temperature, pressure, and volume. The microstate of a system is characterised by the exact configuration of its micro constituents – in classical statistical mechanics, this is the locations and momenta of all of the atoms or other particles. Typically, a macrostate is compatible with many different microstates. We can represent microstates by points in *phase space* – a continuous space containing six dimensions for every particle in the system (one for each direction of position and momentum). Macrostates are represented by regions in phase space. To introduce probabilities, given the laws are deterministic, we will need a probability postulate. Assume a postulate that takes probabilities of volumes of phase space, at a point in time, to be uniform over the standard Lebesgue measure. This implies, roughly, that for any two equally sized volumes of phase space, the system is as likely to be in one as the other.[22]

Using this statistical mechanical framework, we can then derive the probable behaviour for an isolated system in a given macrostate. We consider the region of microstates compatible with its macrostate, apply the probability postulate over this region, and evolve the microstates according to the dynamical laws. We then end up with a probability measure over final *macrostates* of the system, which identifies the probable macro behaviour of the system.

The advantage of this statistical mechanical framework is that it gives us well-defined probabilities for how a macroscopically characterised system will evolve. These probabilities are scientifically respectable, since they play a role in Boltzmannian statistical mechanical explanations of the second law of thermodynamics (the generalisation that systems at non-maximal entropy evolve to higher entropy towards the future). The Boltzmannian entropy of

---

[22] For more on the closely related 'statistical postulate', see Albert (2000: Ch. 4). The use of a probability postulate here does not settle its metaphysics. One might take the postulate to be primitive, reducible to patterns in actual events (perhaps via a best systems analysis) or epistemic in a sense that makes probabilities less real than the fundamental dynamical laws (provided one is willing to accept causal relations that are less real). What is ruled out are taking these probabilities to be temporally or causally asymmetric, as these probabilities must be well defined towards both the temporal and the causal past and future.

a system is given by the measure of microstates compatible with its macrostate. Macrostates with larger measures of compatible microstates have a higher entropy. It turns out that it is overwhelmingly probable that an isolated system at non-maximal entropy will evolve into a higher entropy state. Therefore, we can begin to explain *why* the entropy of isolated systems at non-maximal entropy increases.

Using this statistical mechanical framework, can Lewis' account deliver a probabilistic counterfactual asymmetry? Elga (2001) argues that it cannot. Consider a world that is macroscopically identical to the actual world *after* a small miracle, and so contains almost all of the macroscopic records of an event in the actual world. For example, take the macrostate M_2 at t_2, which contains all of the apparent traces of Nixon having pressed the button at t_1. If we evolve the largest measure of microstates compatible with M_2 back in time, we don't end up in a macrostate in which Nixon presses the button. We instead end up in a world in which Nixon, his aides, the nuclear machinery, and the rest of the Earth at t_2 have evolved in an apparently miraculous and conspiratorial way from a more disordered and *higher* entropy state at t_1. The evolution of the actual world going backwards in time is *extremely* fragile – small changes of the type miracles introduce will mostly lead to worlds with radically different histories from our own. Therefore, local events do not even *probabilistically* determine past events.

Because local events don't probabilistically determine past events, some counterfactual antecedents can easily be satisfied by introducing miracles afterwards. For example, say, in the actual world, Nixon presses the button. The counterfactual antecedent 'it is not the case that Nixon presses the button' can be satisfied by introducing a miracle afterwards, at t_2, such that this nearby world matches the actual world *after* t_2 and is different *before* t_2 (Figure 2). Before t_2, the world has a higher entropy than our own, and Nixon and his aides coalesce only conspiratorially at t_2, implying that it is not the case that Nixon presses the button at t_1. Lewis' recipe leads just as easily to nearby worlds where the past is *different* as to those where the past is the same. Therefore, his account does not imply even a probabilistic temporal asymmetry of counterfactual dependence.

3.3 Albert's and Loewer's Accounts

Recent statistical mechanical accounts of causation share features with Lewis' account. Like Lewis' account, they analyse causation using counterfactual dependence, evaluate counterfactuals using small changes from the actual world, and use an asymmetry of records to explain the temporal asymmetry of causation.

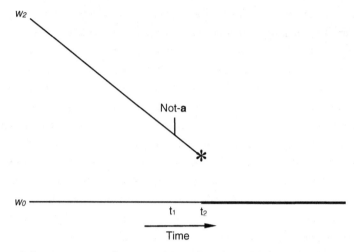

Figure 2 A counterexample to Lewis' explanation of the temporal asymmetry of causation: the actual world (w_0) compared with a nearby possible world (w_2). The worlds match perfectly *after* t_2, at which a small miracle (*) occurs, but are very different prior to t_1.

However, they aim to improve on Lewis' account using resources from statistical mechanics. In this section, I focus on statistical mechanical accounts by David Albert (2000: Ch. 6, 2014, 2015: Ch. 2, 2023) and Barry Loewer (2007, 2012).[23] While neither Albert nor Loewer commits to a particular relation between causation and counterfactuals, they both have something broadly Lewisian in mind.

Statistical mechanical accounts aim to show that earlier events do not counterfactually depend on later events. To avoid Elga's objection, they adopt a different recipe from Lewis for evaluating counterfactuals. First, they stipulate that nearby counterfactual worlds must *begin* in the same *particular* low-entropy macrostate that the actual universe began in. Albert calls this postulate the 'past hypothesis' (Albert, 2000: 96).[24] This postulate is motivated by the fact that low-entropy initial states feature in Boltzmannian statistical mechanical explanations of thermodynamic asymmetries (Reichenbach, 1956; Feynman, 1965; Horwich, 1987; Sklar, 1993: Ch. 10; Albert, 2000, 2015; Loewer, 2007, 2012).[25] Second, these accounts

---

[23] Kutach (2002, 2007) considers a similar account. Reichenbach (1956) defends a distinct statistical mechanical account, considered in Section 5.2.

[24] The past hypothesis is about the *particular* state that the universe begun in – not merely its being low entropy (Albert, 2000: 96). The past hypothesis will need to be amended if the concept of entropy does not apply at the start of the universe or if the universe has no beginning (Albert, 2000: 85; Earman, 2006: 412).

[25] For objections, see Leeds (2003), Earman (2006), and Maudlin (2007).

invoke the statistical postulate – this is similar to the probability measure over microstates compatible with a given macrostate set out in Section 3.2, but is applied only to the initial state of the universe. This postulate is also justified by its use in statistical mechanical explanations. These two postulates, combined with the dynamical laws, imply that the entropy of nearby counterfactual worlds will increase towards the future – in accord with what we expect from the second law of thermodynamics.

Using these postulates, Albert gives the following recipe for evaluating counterfactuals. Take the location of the actual world in phase space at the time of the antecedent – where points in phase space specify the position and momentum of all particles at a given time (Section 3.2). The nearest counterfactual world satisfies the following requirements:

1. The counterfactual antecedent is true.
2. The fundamental dynamical laws are those of the actual world.
3. The past hypothesis is true.
4. The world's macro history, given its macrostate at the time of the antecedent and the past hypothesis, is assigned a reasonable probability by the statistical postulate.
5. The state of the counterfactual world at the time of the antecedent is as near as possible to the state of the actual world, as measured in phase space, consistent with satisfying the other requirements.

A counterfactual is true if and only if its consequent is satisfied in the nearest counterfactual world. Here's an example. Say, in the actual world, you're holding a glass of water. Consider the counterfactual: if you were to tip the glass over, water would spill out. To evaluate this counterfactual, consider all of the worlds in which you tip the glass (requirement 1). Reject worlds that have different fundamental dynamical laws from the actual world (requirement 2). Reject 'conspiratorial' worlds that begin in high-entropy states (requirement 3). Reject worlds that have very unlikely conspiratorial behaviour at any time, and so have unlikely macro histories given their macrostate now (requirement 4).[26] Finally, minimise changes from the actual world by picking the *nearest* world in phase space to the actual world at the time of the antecedent – the world that involves the least differences in particle positions and momenta (requirement 5). The expectation is that the dynamical laws at this nearest world will imply that water spills out after the glass is tipped over. Therefore, the counterfactual is

---

[26] Albert's initial statement of his account (2000: 96, 128–30) is ambiguous between the above interpretation and one that rules out *any* changes to the macrostate of the world at the time of the antecedent outside the antecedent. For the latter interpretation, see Frisch (2007: 381). For reasons considered in Section 3.6, Albert (2023) now prefers the above interpretation.

true. Albert's initial claim is that many future-directed counterfactuals like this turn out to be true, but hardly any past-directed counterfactuals do.

Loewer (2007) defends a similar account.[27] However, Loewer's recipe, rather than picking out a *single* nearest world (requirement 5) with statistically normal behaviour (requirement 4), instead uses a *probability measure* (the statistical postulate) over a *volume* of nearby worlds – those whose *macrostate* at the time of the antecedent does not differ from that of the actual world outside the area of the antecedent.[28] On Loewer's account, counterfactuals will typically have probabilistic consequents. If you were to tip the glass, it is merely highly probable that water would spill out. Loewer's initial claim is that many future-directed counterfactuals like this have high-probability consequents, but hardly any past-directed counterfactuals.

Albert's and Loewer's attempts to derive a counterfactual asymmetry depend on the claim that the past hypothesis implies an asymmetry of 'records' (Albert, 2000: Ch. 6, 2014, 2015: Ch. 2; Loewer, 2007, 2012). Records, in Albert's technical sense, are local states of a system at one time that are reliably correlated with the state of a system (itself or another) at another time, given the dynamical laws, the past hypothesis, and the statistical postulate. While local states are not enough to guarantee that events at other times occur, given the dynamical laws alone (Section 2.2), Albert and Loewer argue that local events are enough to probabilistically determine other events, given the dynamical laws, the statistical postulate, and the past hypothesis. (One may also wish to include background information.) Albert argues that there can be records of the past because the past hypothesis provides a constraint on the past. When reasoning about the past, you reason to a state that lies at a time *between* two constrained states – the past hypothesis and whatever states you know in the present. Reasoning in this way is much more informative than reasoning from a single state.[29] However, there is no future hypothesis that provides a similar constraint about the future.

Albert and Loewer argue that the asymmetry of records implies an asymmetry of counterfactual dependence. Because their recipes for evaluating counterfactuals require minimising or eliminating macroscopic changes from the actual world at the time of the antecedent, counterfactual worlds will, at the time of the antecedent, contain almost all of the records there are in the actual world

---

[27] Loewer (2012) defends a variant that uses probabilities rather than counterfactuals.

[28] Kutach (2002) considers a related proposal in which the *microstate* outside a given region is held fixed (Kutach, 2002, 2007). Kutach's later account (Kutach, 2013: Chs. 6 and 7) uses a similar kind of screening off as Loewer's account, combined with an agential argument that rules out direct control of the past. See Blanchard (2015) for discussion.

[29] Arguably, what ultimately underwrites Albert's record asymmetry is the fact that the world is on an entropy slope (Fernandes, 2022b). For concerns regarding Albert's account, see Leeds (2003) and Frisch (2007).

of the actual past. In the Nixon case, the relevant nearby counterfactual worlds will contain Nixon's memories, a signal in the wire, and so forth. If Albert and Loewer are right about records, these local events are enough, given the dynamical laws, the statistical postulate, and the past hypothesis, to determine (or at least make it very likely) that Nixon presses the button. If so, it seems that recorded events will not counterfactually depend on later antecedents. However, no similar argument can be made regarding future events. Because there are no records of the future, small changes of the kind that counterfactual antecedents introduce may lead to large changes to future states. Therefore, the future depends counterfactually on the present in a way that the past does not.

Before continuing, it's worth being clear on the structure of Albert's and Loewer's argument. Their argument depends crucially on our methods of evaluating counterfactuals mirroring how we infer using records. If inferring using records works via the same procedure as we use when evaluating counterfactuals, and if nearby worlds contain the same present records as the actual world, then whatever events those records are *of* will also be the same in nearby counterfactual worlds. Since there are records of the past and not the future, past events are held fixed in a way that future events are not.

Albert's and Loewer's accounts have several advantages over Lewis' account. First, many have found miracles unpalatable (Dorr, 2016). Albert's and Loewer's recipes avoid Lewis' miracles, since they keep the fundamental dynamical laws unchanged. Second, because Albert and Loewer use posits that feature in scientific explanations, such as the past hypothesis and the statistical postulate, their recipe has some scientific justification. Third, because their accounts relate the temporal asymmetry of causation to other temporal asymmetries, they help unify these phenomena. Overall, it seems that Albert and Loewer give a *scientific* explanation of the temporal asymmetry of causation.

3.4 Bells and Whistles

As they stand, however, Albert's and Loewer's accounts don't imply a strict asymmetry of counterfactual dependence. Additions must be made. I'll begin with the least controversial additions and consider more controversial additions in Section 3.6. The general form of these additions is to accept that there may be counterfactual dependence of the past on the present, but to argue that this doesn't constitute a significant form of causation or 'control'.

First, statistical mechanical accounts must restrict counterfactual consequents. Because the laws are kept intact, any counterfactual change to the present necessarily implies changes to the *microstate* of the past, which might be picked out using gerrymandered macro variables. If microscopic consequents (or gerrymandered variables) are allowed, the past may counterfactually depend on the present. Albert restricts counterfactual consequents to local macroscopic states of affairs that concern a 'relatively small and unisolated subsystem of the world ... and which can be expressed in a relatively simple, natural, straightforward, everyday sort of language' (Albert, 2000: 122, No. 11). Loewer allows for microscopic consequents, but argues that counterfactual dependence of past microstates will not amount to a significant form of 'control' because we can't know about the micro correlations that obtain (Loewer, 2007: 318). These restrictions are reasonable if causation is primarily a macroscopic phenomenon.[30]

Second, Albert's and Loewer's accounts must restrict the counterfactual *antecedents* to relatively small, localised areas. If antecedents are large, or very diverse, then there may be counterfactual dependence of the past on the present. For example, a large antecedent such as 'all humans have tattoos on 1 January 2023' would require some changes to events prior to allow everyone to non-miraculously acquire tattoos. Albert restricts the antecedents using a 'fiction of agency': a 'primitive and un-argued-for and not-to-be-further-analyzed conception' of what features are thought of as falling under our '*direct* and *unproblematical* and *unmediated* control' (Albert, 2000: 128). This 'black box' conception can be filled in in various ways – to give us direct control of our limbs, for example, or the electrical nerve impulses in our brains. Albert claims that under any reasonable conception, our direct control will be localised to a very small area of the universe. Loewer restricts the antecedents to decisions, actions, or a combination of both (Loewer, 2007: 316–17, 2012: 127).

These restrictions to the antecedents are more problematic. First, they are in tension with the aspiration of statistical mechanical accounts to provide a (purely) scientific account of causation. Instead, we find these accounts adopting features of agency accounts (Section 4). Second, these restrictions limit counterfactual antecedents to decisions or events that we control directly, whereas we presumably want to derive counterfactual and causal relations obtaining between other events. On this point, statistical mechanical accounts face the same concern as agency accounts. I discuss possible solutions in Sections 3.7 and 4.6. Given these difficulties, one might replace these agential restrictions with a restriction to localised areas. This response will alleviate the present concerns. In Sections 3.6 and 3.7, I'll return to the question of whether statistical mechanical accounts can avoid appeals to agency.

---

[30] See Section 4.1 for similar restrictions in the case of agency accounts. For further discussions, see Arntzenius (1990), Sklar (1993: 346 ff.), Pearl (2000: 59), Field (2003), and Woodward (2007: 89).

3.5 Objection 1: Causation in All Settings

Various concerns have been raised against statistical mechanical accounts (Sklar, 1993; Earman, 2006; Price and Weslake, 2009; Frisch, 2010). I will consider two kinds that are relevant for the attempt by statistical mechanical accounts to explain the temporal asymmetry of causation.

First, some have worried that statistical mechanical accounts can't deliver a temporal asymmetry of causation between microstates or in settings lacking an entropic asymmetry or where the entropic asymmetry is reversed – the latter might be other possible worlds or parts of our own universe (Price, 1996: Ch. 6, 2007).

In response, Albert and Loewer could simply deny that there is a temporal asymmetry of causation (or even causation) in these cases. While it might *seem* that causation is temporally asymmetric at the micro level or in universes lacking entropic asymmetry, these are intuitions about causation that we should give up. I suggested earlier (Section 2.4) that treating the temporal asymmetry of causation as a purely macroscopic phenomenon is plausible. Furthermore, given Russell's second argument (Section 2.2), it is not surprising if what causal relations obtain is sensitive to surrounding entropic structure (for related arguments, see Field (2003)). While one would still need to explain why we *think* there would be a temporal asymmetry of causation in cases lacking entropic asymmetry, it is no surprise if our intuitions are poor guides to such cases, given how pervasive entropic asymmetry is.

As a second response, one could attempt to derive the temporal asymmetry of causation in these cases from the macroscopic entropic asymmetry of our world (that obtains around here and now); for a related response, see Weslake (2006: 248). This response would require supplementing the statistical mechanical account with a 'projectivist' component – the direction of causation is projected in cases that lack entropic asymmetry, but that are still temporally oriented with respect to our entropic asymmetry. While Price seems to think that such a response would require giving up a statistical mechanical account, it would leave statistical mechanical accounts' core explanation of the temporal asymmetry of causation intact. While I prefer the first response, following Reichenbach (1956), both are available under statistical mechanical accounts.

3.6 Objection 2: Backwards Counterfactual Dependence

More troubling are counterexamples where the statistical mechanical recipe seems to imply that earlier events counterfactually depend on later events. If these counterexamples succeed, it seems that statistical mechanical accounts won't deliver an asymmetry of counterfactual dependence or the temporal asymmetry of causation. There are three kinds of counterexample.

The first kind of counterexample, due to Elga (2001) and Kutach (2002), are cases where there are no records of a past macroscopic event at the time of the antecedent.[31] Say Atlantis sunk many years ago, and there are no records now of Atlantis' existence. The probability that Atlantis existed, given the present macrostate of the universe, the past hypothesis, and the statistical postulate, is, therefore, very low. Consider the counterfactual antecedent 'you move your finger at t_1' given that you don't move your finger. Because there are no records of Atlantis' existence at t_1, the statistical mechanical recipe will *not* imply that any such records are kept intact in nearby counterfactual worlds. Without records to keep the past state intact, the relevantly nearby counterfactual worlds may well be those in which Atlantis never existed (Albert) or in which the probability of Atlantis having existed is extremely low (Loewer). Without records, the past is extremely fragile with respect to small changes in the present. Given the fact that we control small changes in the present, statistical mechanical accounts seem to imply that we can control past macrostates as well.

Albert (2014, 2015: Ch. 2) and Loewer (2012: 128) respond to this case by introducing further conditions on what counts as the right kind of counterfactual dependence for *control*.[32] Control, they argue, requires counterfactual dependence that we can *know* about. We can't know about the correlations between the movement of a finger now and the existence of Atlantis – the evidence of Atlantis' existence is hidden in the present microstate. There can't be macroscopic correlations because, if there were, there would be records of Atlantis' existence in the present.

A second kind of counterexample, due to Frisch (2010), are cases where there is only one record of a past event in the present and that record is under the agent's direct control. Say you're playing a piano piece and come to a point in the music where you can decide whether to play the first or second ending – the decision being under your direct control. Stipulate that you have no memory of what music you have played and there are no external records. However, you are a reliable pianist. Whatever decision you make *counts* as a record of what music you have played. Therefore, by having control of your decision in the present and your decision being a unique record, you have

---

[31] The case is based on claims by Elga (2001) and is cited as Elga's in Loewer (2007: 318–19, 2012: 128).

[32] Loewer (2007: 318) also notes that the probability of Atlantis' existence doesn't change between the actual world and the counterfactual world.

control over the past. This control is presumably of a kind you could come to know about; therefore, Albert's and Loewer's first response is not available.

Loewer's account avoids this counterexample, and a third kind of counter-example (discussed later in this section), by stipulating that decisions are never correlated with previous macrostates.[33] Loewer takes decisions to be, *by defin-ition*, uncorrelated with previous macrostates (2007: 317, 2012). If so, decisions can never be records of past events. However, this definition introduces an unexplained asymmetry, namely that decisions are probabilistically independ-ent of past (but not future) macrostates. This is an assumption that we are not entitled to if we are to explain the temporal asymmetry of causation.

Albert at first dismisses such cases, claiming that records are 'manifestly *not* things that can by any stretch of the imagination be thought of as ... under our *direct* and *unmediated* and *unproblematical control*' (Albert, 2000: 130). However, while many records are not under our direct control, our decisions are. In cases where our decisions are reliable responses to the past, they count as records of the past. Later, Albert (2014) suggests that *effective* control of the past requires that one's influence of the past brings additional future gains beyond what one could simply have by influencing the present. In the Frisch (2010) case, influencing the past (what music you have played) doesn't bring you any additional gains beyond what you had by influencing the present (your present playing). This response, however, also relies on an unexplained asymmetry – effective control of the *past* must have further implications for the *future*, while effective control of the *future* doesn't have to have further implications for the *past*. Moreover, this response can't deal with a third kind of counterexample, considered below.

Fernandes (2023) suggests a different response. To effectively control the past, it is not enough to know that, in general, your decisions are correlated with past events. To effectively control the past, you must have some way of checking whether you have controlled it, in similar cases where you *attempt* to do so. You cannot do this in the Frisch case – because your decision in the present is the only record of the past event, there is no time at which you can know both your decision and the past event by independent means. Therefore, you cannot determine whether you have controlled the past in this or similar cases where you attempt to do so.

A third kind of counterexample (Fernandes, 2023) was designed to evade even this response. The counterexample concerns a case where your decision is a record of a past event, but there is also *another* record of that past event not

---

[33] Loewer (2007: 318) also relies on this stipulation to make an additional response to the first counterexample. This response is problematic for the reasons I explore later in this section.

under your direct control. Say, in the actual world, a fly flies in front of your face at t_1 and at t_2 you swat it away. Consider the counterfactual: if you had not swatted at t_2, the fly would have been somewhere else at t_1. Stipulate that you are an exceedingly reliable fly-swatter, well trained to swat away flies whenever they appear. If so, your decision to swat is a *record* of the fly's location. Consider that there are no other records of the fly's location in the present, except the fly itself and a tiny recording device that tracks its location. Using Albert's recipe, you can control the fly's location in the past because you directly control your decision, your decision is a record of the fly's location, and the other records of the fly's location are small – and so they can easily change in counterfactual worlds. The recording device allows you to determine whether you have controlled the past. The device even allows you to be rewarded in the future for doing so.

This 'fly case' relies on the fly-swatter, the fly, and the recording devices remaining 'reliable' in counterfactual scenarios, such that their present and past states in the counterfactual scenario remain correlated. We don't reason to counterfactual scenarios where the fly-swatter ignores the fly or the recording device breaks down. The case exploits a positive feature of Albert's account: that it aims to keep records reliable. If Albert's recipe allowed for records to easily be misleading, we would lose the argument that the recorded past remains intact. Requirement 4 does much of the work of ruling out misleading records: that the world's macro history, given its macrostate and the past hypothesis, is assigned a reasonable probability by the statistical postulate. This requirement rules out correlations that aren't in accord with macroscopic dynamics of the kind we're familiar with and that, even once the past hypothesis is conditionalised on, are 'hidden' in microstates. The requirement for a reasonably probable macro history means that changes to the present state can be accommodated, if they are needed to keep the macro history sufficiently probable.

While Albert doesn't specify how probable the macro history needs to be, there are reasons to think that satisfying requirement 4 will require changes to be allowed to the present of the kind that the fly case exploits. First, Albert defends his requirements by arguing that they capture our 'normal procedures of inference' (Albert, 2000: 130). It is normal to infer across local states at a single time. My morning newspaper allows me to infer the contents of yours. Capturing this inference, if my paper had been different, yours would have been as well. For this counterfactual to be true, and for newspapers to remain reliable, Albert's method must allow for macroscopic changes outside the antecedent. Second, the fly case can be enriched by adding in records of the reliability of the relevant devices, that is, large records that are more difficult to change, given Albert's recipe, than the small records that the devices produce. These large records, remaining unchanged, add to the improbability of the macro histories in which the devices are unreliable.

As noted, Loewer's account avoids this counterexample by requiring decisions to be probabilistically uncorrelated with previous macrostates. For the reasons given earlier, that response is problematic. There's a second way in which Loewer's account avoids the counterexample. Loewer (2007: 317) requires that decisions are probabilistically uncorrelated with *present* macrostates, that is, macrostates outside the spatial area of the antecedent at the time of the antecedent. This requirement rules out the location of the fly at t_2 (or the recording device) changing in counterfactual worlds. While Loewer's requirement is not temporally asymmetric, it is problematic for two other reasons. First, it rules out simultaneous counterfactual dependence by *fiat*, rather than allowing whether it obtains to be an empirical contingency (see Price and Weslake, 2009: 426; Frisch, 2010: 29; Albert, 2023). Second, Loewer's requirement rules out probabilistic dependencies that we find in the actual world. There are cases where our decisions are correlated with past and present macroscopic states, such as when your decision to buy a chocolate ice cream is correlated with the presence of an ice cream van. For further arguments, see Fernandes (2022a).

How else might we respond? Albert (2015: 49–50) argues that our control of the past in the Frisch and fly cases is not suitably *robust*. Robust correlations are those that can be employed for a variety of reasons. Similarly, Fernandes (2023) suggests that robust correlations are those that still hold when one attempts to use them for gain. The control in the Frisch and fly cases is not robust in either of these senses, since it relies on the agent's decision being a reliable response to the past event, rather than to their desires or intentions. A response of this kind is central to agent-based explanations of the temporal asymmetry of causation and will be evaluated in Sections 4.4 and 4.6. Crucial to its success will be showing that it can be given in non-causal terms.

While the Frisch and fly cases took some time to develop, they were, in a sense, inevitable – they are examples of backwards counterfactual dependence during the transition period. While Albert's and Loewer's accounts do away with Lewis' miracles, they still have *macroscopic* transition periods, that is, times, prior to the antecedent, where the counterfactual world diverges macroscopically from the actual world. A macroscopic transition period is inevitable if one wishes to minimise disruptions to *macroscopic* regularities. What gives statistical mechanical accounts new resources for answering the problem of the transition period is their introducing agency. However, the introduction of agency raises problems as well – we'll consider these next.

3.7 The Role of Agency

There are several ways in which statistical mechanical accounts invoke agency: the restriction of antecedents to decisions or events we control directly (Section 3.4) and the restriction of correlations to *knowable* and *robust* control (Section 3.6). Are these appeals to agency problematic?

First, one might worry that appealing to agency will compromise the objectivity of the explanation of the temporal asymmetry of causation. To my mind, it is no compromise to objectivity to use agency to explain features of the world that are relevant to agents – as agency accounts do (Section 4.2). However, for those looking for an *alternative* to agency accounts, the appearance of agency in statistical mechanical accounts is concerning.

Second, once statistical mechanical accounts introduce agency, they face problems that beset agency accounts. One such problem is that, by restricting counterfactual antecedents to decisions or events that we control directly, there is no account of the temporal asymmetry of causation for events we don't, or can't, control. The responses adopted by agency accounts will be discussed in Section 4.6. An alternative response is to apply the statistical mechanical recipe for evaluating counterfactuals to non-agential antecedents. As noted in Section 3.4, we might restrict antecedents to small, localised areas. While this does provide a more objective account of causation, it removes the agential resources that statistical mechanical accounts use to respond to the counterexamples considered in Section 3.6. In fact, counterexamples become easier to generate. In any case, where a counterfactual antecedent is the only or one of the few records of a past event, the Frisch or fly counterexamples can be generated. While it might seem strange to think of an agent's decisions as records, we often *expect* states of ordinary objects to be records – such as photographs and recordings. These states may also record events from long ago. If so, the transition period may be very long indeed, implying widespread backwards counterfactual dependence.

A third consequence of appealing to agency is that the asymmetric probability structure of the world turns out to play less of a role in explaining the temporal asymmetry of causation than we might have wanted, given the aspirations of statistical mechanical accounts. The way statistical mechanical accounts are presented, the asymmetries of statistical mechanics imply counterfactuals that are for the most part temporally asymmetric – and considerations of agency are only introduced to deal with *recherche* counterexamples. However, the responses made to these counterexamples, if they're successful, are enough to explain the temporal asymmetry of causation, without having to go via a for-the-most part counterfactual asymmetry (Fernandes, 2016b: 203–18; Loew, 2017; see also Beebee, 2015, for related concerns). I return to this point in

Section 5.1. While the probability structure still plays a role in explaining the temporal asymmetry of causation (Section 4.6), there is no longer a straight line from an asymmetric probability structure to an asymmetry of causation.

Despite the concerns, there is an advantage to statistical mechanical accounts adopting features of agency. As noted in Section 3.2, one issue with Lewis' account is that, because it is reverse engineered to deliver the temporal asymmetry of causation, it provides no deep understanding of why causal relations are temporally asymmetric or why counterfactuals are useful to us (Bennett, 1984; Horwich, 1987: 172; Woodward, 2003: 137). Given the use of causation for choosing effective strategies (Section 2.4), it seems there should be some justification for why causal relations, evaluated using a particular counterfactual recipe, are able to play their role (Price and Weslake, 2009).

The three agency-related restrictions used by statistical mechanical accounts go some way to answering these concerns. They guarantee that causal relations will concern antecedents that are controllable and relations that are knowable and exploitable for gain. However, there are other aspects of the statistical mechanical recipe to requiring that require justification, including the use of the dynamical laws, the statistical postulate, and the past hypothesis. Loewer (2007: 304–6) justifies these posits by noting that they are all laws, under his Humean 'best systems' account of lawhood. However, there are problems with this justification. Under a Humean 'best systems' account, laws derive from the best systematisations of actual events. Given that they're just ways of summarising information about actual events, it is unclear, prima facie, why they should be held fixed when evaluating counterfactuals, which are about non-actual events. Nor does this appeal work for other requirements of Loewer's recipe, such as keeping the area outside the antecedent fixed.

A more promising approach is Albert's suggestion that his counterfactual recipe captures our 'normal procedures of inference' (Albert, 2000: 129; see also Loewer, 2012: 126–7). Insofar as a recipe is based on what underlies our reasoning about even hypothetical local states, we have some account of why the recipe is appropriate when reasoning counterfactually. Such a move brings statistical mechanical accounts even closer to agency accounts, particularly those using objective probabilities (Section 4.2).

Having seen how far statistical mechanical accounts adopt features of agency, it is time to evaluate agency accounts on their own terms.

4 Agency Accounts

Agency accounts make sense of causal relations by relating them to effective strategies (Section 4.1). While they offer different accounts of what causal relations *are* (Section 4.2), they all agree that causal relations must be useful for agents deciding what to do. Agency accounts also use features of agents to explain why causes come prior in time to their effects; in addition, they claim that their ability to explain the temporal asymmetry of causation is a major advantage. Huw Price, for example, argues that deliberation 'undermines' correlations between an agent's actions now and past events, implying that there will be no backwards causation in real-world cases (Section 4.3). However, Price's explanation turns out to rely on causal features of deliberation (Section 4.4). Other agency accounts attempt non-causal explanations for why correlations to the past are undermined by deliberation (Section 4.5). These have better prospects for explaining the temporal asymmetry of causation, although they must also appeal to features of worldly structure (Section 4.6).

4.1 The Core of Agency Accounts

The core motivation for agency accounts is that there is a connection between causal relations and effective strategies (see Section 2.4 and Cartwright (1979)). Knowing about causal relations allows agents to know what correlations will help them achieve the outcomes that they seek. Different accounts of causation, including interventionist accounts (Pearl, 2000; Woodward, 2003), agree that there is a connection between causation and effective strategies. What distinguishes agency accounts is that they explicitly use the link between causation and effective strategies to identify, elucidate, or otherwise make sense of causal relations – and to explain their temporal asymmetry. Agency accounts may acknowledge that causation plays other useful roles, such as in explanation and prediction. However, it's the use of causation in choosing effective strategies that is causation's core role. Because the effective-strategies role is defined by reference to *agents* (creatures who deliberate and act), agency features in the account of causation.

Early defenders of agency accounts include Ramsey ([1929] 1978) (perhaps), Collingwood (1940: 296–312), Gasking (1955), von Wright (1971: Ch. 2), and Dieks (1986). Recent defenders include Price (1991, 1992a, 1992b, 1996, 2007, 2012, 2017), Menzies and Price (1993), van Fraassen (1993), Hitchcock (1996), Weslake (2006), Eagle (2007), Ismael (2007, 2012, 2013, 2016), Menzies (2007), Price and Weslake (2009), Blanchard (2014), Beebee (2015), Fernandes (2017, 2023), and Evans (2020). For general discussions of agency accounts, see Hausman (1997), Woodward (2003, 2016), and Blanchard (2016).

According to recent defenders of agency accounts, the role of causation in choosing effective strategies implies a relation between causation and probabilities of relevance to deliberating agents. In Price's formulation (1992b: 261), 'If in the context of means-end deliberation to realise **A** as the immediate product of a free action would be to raise the probability of **B**, then **B** is thought of as an effect of **A**.' Fernandes (2017: 691) and Blanchard (2014) defend similar biconditionals. In Fernandes' probabilistic formulation (2017: 702, No. 19), **A** is causally relevant to **B** *if and only if* an agent deciding **A** (in proper deliberation) for the sake of **B** would raise the probability of **B**, compared with not deciding on **A**, where the relevant probabilities are conditional on the agent's evidence while deliberating.

Causes raise the probability of their effects when they are 'brought about' in a free and immediate way as the outcome of deliberation. For example, smoking causes lung cancer if and only if someone freely deciding to smoke raises their probability of their developing lung cancer. Since agents are interested in raising the probability of intended outcomes by their free acts, they need causal information.

Part of the motivation for agency accounts is that they give a straightforward answer to why we should care about causal relations. If causal relations are those correlations we can use to achieve outcomes we seek, no wonder we care about them. Agency accounts neatly answer the problems concerning justification (Section 3.2) and counterexamples (Section 3.4) raised against counterfactual and statistical mechanical accounts by explicitly building in conditions on what correlations count as causal – they are those that agents can make use of.

The need for causal relations to be relevant to deliberating agents induces three restrictions on the causal relata. First, the cause, **A**, must be a 'direct option' – an action, event, or state that an agent can decide upon or achieve 'immediately' without having to first decide on or achieve something else. Chu's moving his hand may be a direct option, whereas his completing his assignment is more likely to be an indirect option. This restriction to direct options is justified by the effective-strategies role. Agents are more interested in what their direct options imply, since direct options can be achieved more reliably than indirect options. Strategies involving indirect options can be formulated by combining strategies involving direct options.

Second, the effect, **B**, must be something an agent could plausibly know about and be interested in. If one is allowed to gerrymander effect variables, one will always be able to generate cases of backwards causation, as with other accounts of causation (Section 3.4). Within agency accounts, the restriction to non-gerrymandered variables is motivated by the abilities and interests of agents.

Third, the agent's decision or deliberation on **A** must be (or must be taken to be) 'free'. An agent's decision or deliberating being free typically implies that the agent can decide on **A** or some incompatible option (not-**A**) or takes it she can do so. She has more than one incompatible 'available' option. A minimal condition on an option being available is that the agent can raise the subjective or objective probability of that option through her decision, given her evidence. If an agent is to have several incompatible available options, her evidence while she deliberates can't settle how she decides. For some (Fernandes, 2016a), engaging in free deliberation requires an agent not to already have evidence that settles how she'll decide. For others (Ismael, 2007), a deliberating agent is epistemically unconstrained by apparent evidence of how she'll decide.

The requirements on free decision or deliberation might be primitive or justified by appeal to empirical facts, normative facts, or some combination of the two. In the case of justifying why free decisions are evidentially unsettled, one might appeal to the complexity of decision-making (empirical) or the waste of cognitive resources in deliberating on a known outcome (normative). For further discussions of these options, see Ismael (2007, 2012) and Fernandes (2016a, 2017).[34] We'll see the work that these three requirements do in explaining the temporal asymmetry of causation in Sections 4.3–4.6.

4.2 What Are Causal Relations?

While recent agency accounts agree that there is a connection between causation and probabilities of relevance to deliberating agents, they use this link in different ways and offer different accounts of what causal relations are and why causes come before their effects.

Price defends a *perspectivalist* account of causation (1991, 1992a, 1992b, 1996, 2007, 2012, 2017; see also Menzies and Price, 1993; Price and Weslake, 2009; Beebee, 2015). It is only when we take up the point of view of a deliberating agent that causation appears in our worldview. Causation is in this sense 'perspectival'. Causal relations hold 'from the free agent's distinctive point of view' (Price, 1991: 173) or are 'assessed from the agent's distinctive epistemic perspective' (Price, 2012: 494). The deliberating agent has a particular epistemic stance on the world because she takes her decisions to be probabilistically independent of everything except their effects. Therefore, if we look at things from her perspective, there aren't probabilistic relations between her decisions now and their causes.

In early work, Menzies and Price (1993) characterised this as a 'response-dependent' account. In the same way that the concept of the colour RED depends on our responses to red objects, the concept CAUSATION depends on our engagements as agents. While in later work, Price (2017) distanced himself

---

[34] One might appeal to the idea that the effective strategies that causal relations pick out must be *robust* – those that can be employed for a variety of reasons and in a variety of circumstances (see Section 3.6, Albert (2015: 49–50), and Fernandes (2023)). One way to achieve such robustness is to model an agent's decisions as evidentially disconnected from certain states.

from this formulation, he maintains that understanding CAUSATION requires acknowledging its perspectival character. Price most often considers himself to be concerned with giving a *functional genealogy* to causal concepts: 'not an account of what causation is, but an account of how we come to speak in causal terms' (Price, 1992a: 518) and 'what function it serves in our lives' (Price, 1992a: 519). He describes his project as 'philosophical anthropology' (Price, 2017: 75; see also Price, 2007, 2017; Price and Weslake, 2009). We come to speak in causal terms because causal concepts are useful in identifying what we take to be effective strategies. Saying 'A causes B', according to Price, is a way of *expressing* one's subjective conditional probabilities concerning B, given one freely decides on A. Altogether, the relation between causation and effective strategies tells us about the function, genealogy, and use conditions of the *concept* of causation. It does not provide an analysis or account of causation itself. According to Price, the question about what causal relations *are* is not amenable to philosophical investigation.

Ismael (2007, 2013, 2016) agrees with Price about the genealogy and function of our causal concepts. However, she argues (Ismael, 2016) that features of agency do not feature as part of the content or truth conditions of causal claims, as Price's account might suggest. Ismael adopts, instead, an interventionist account of the truth conditions of causal claims. While Price and Ismael differ in their accounts of the concept CAUSATION, neither is interested in providing an agency account of what causal relations *are*.

Blanchard (2014) and Fernandes (2017), by contrast, develop agency accounts of what causal relations *are*. They use features of agents to pick out certain objective worldly structures as causal, claiming a correspondence between causal relations and objective probabilistic relations that are effective strategies for deliberating agents.[35] Blanchard (2014) uses this correspondence to reduce causal relations to objective worldly probabilities. Fernandes (2017) is more cautious, arguing for a correspondence between causal relations and probabilities. However, if one is willing to identify objective probabilities that provide reasons for belief as objective *worldly* probabilities, these accounts agree on what causal relations obtain.

Agency accounts have different aims and use 'probability' in different senses. In order to be able to talk generally about agency accounts, I'll use 'probability' to refer neutrally to both subjective and objective probabilities, unless stated otherwise.

---

[35] As with statistical mechanical accounts, these probabilities might be primitive, reducible to non-modal structure, or epistemic (provided one is willing to accept causal relations that are similarly epistemic). They must be well defined towards both the causal and the temporal past and future.

4.3 Explaining the Temporal Asymmetry of Causation

Agency accounts aim to explain the temporal asymmetry of causation. A quick argument suggests that, if causation is related to effective strategies, causal relations in our world will be temporally asymmetric. Consider an agent deliberating on whether to do **A** to achieve **B**, in the sense of raising **B**'s probability. Will it ever be reasonable for her to decide on **A** to achieve **B** if **B** lies in the past? It seems not. One apparent feature of the world is that it is never reasonable to decide on options now to raise the probability of past outcomes. We can regret past outcomes, but we never plan on doing things now to 'ensure' past events. If one adopts an agency account of causation, it seems there won't be causal relations directed towards the past in our world. Prima facie, agency accounts seem to *imply* the temporal asymmetry of causation.

However, there are two immediate problems with this quick explanation. First, it may be true that our actions now, **A**, don't raise the probability of events prior to our deliberation. However, they may well raise the probability of events temporally between our decision and action. Deciding to do **A**, or doing **A**, raises the probability of whatever events are required to bring about one doing **A**. For example, Chu's moving his hand *raises* the probability of certain muscles in his arm contracting. However, his moving his hand doesn't *cause* those muscles to contract. This objection is akin to the problem of backwards coun-terfactual dependence in the 'transition period' (Sections 3.2 and 3.6). Hausman (1997) and Woodward (2016: Section 3) raise related problems – without further conditions, agency accounts will sometimes count spurious correlations (such as when **A** and **B** are common effects) as causal. Price might be thought to avoid this result by taking **A** to be the 'immediate product' of deliberation (Price, 1992b: 261). However, unless we are prepared to limit *all* causes to decisions, agency accounts need another way of ruling out such correlations as causal.

One might respond by arguing that there is deficiency on the part of agents when they decide on events, actions, or states to achieve their causal precondi-tions (Fernandes, 2017). If Chu wants to contract his muscles, he should just do so – rather than raising his hand as a means of doing so. Ordinary cases where we decide on an option to bring abouts its preconditions seem to involve deficiencies in motivation or control – such as if one decides to post a letter in order to get some exercise. Arguably, the causal intermediary (getting some exercise) should be able to be brought about more reliably than the putative cause (posting a letter), given the probabilistic structure of the world. It seems that we should decide on the more reliable to bring about the less reliable, not the other way around. Regardless of how one responds, note that this is a problem for any account that uses a link between causation and effective strategies – it seems there are effective strategies (deciding on actions to ensure their preconditions) that aren't causal.[36]

A second concern with this putative explanation is that, even if an asymmetry in effective strategies *implies* the temporal asymmetry of causation, it may not *explain* the temporal asymmetry of causation. There may instead be a causal explanation for why agents should never deliberate to achieve past outcomes. Perhaps (a) causation's temporal asymmetry is primitive or explained in some non-agency way and (b) agents should decide on direct options that they take to be *causally relevant* to outcomes they seek. 'Causal decision theory' is committed to (b).

A first step in defending an agent-based *explanation* of causation's temporal asymmetry is to argue that we can model how agents should decide in *evidential* terms, rather than *causal* terms – so, we don't have to assume (b). According to 'evidential decision theory', reasonable deliberators decide on direct options that are *evidence* of outcomes they seek, in the sense that they raise the subjective probability of those outcomes. If evidential decision theory is right, perhaps effective strategies can be identified as those that raise the probability of intended outcomes, and the agency theorist can identify *those* correlations as causal. Causal decision theorists, by contrast, argue that deciding on options that merely raise the probability of outcomes will lead to incorrect recommendations (Skyrms, 1980; Lewis, 1981a; Jackson and Pargetter, 1983).

Price's account is the most developed attempt to use evidential decision theory to give an agent-based explanation of the temporal asymmetry of causation. Price intends to explain why agents *take* causation to be temporally asymmetric – which is the appropriate explanandum, given his perspectivalism. I'll consider Price's explanation in this section and the next and I will consider alternatives in Sections 4.5 and 4.6. Price (1986) (see also Price, 1991, 1992b, 2007, 2012; Menzies and Price, 1993; Price and Weslake, 2009; Beebee, 2015) argues that evidential decision theory can explain why agents should never decide on direct options now to achieve past outcomes in typical real-world cases. The limit to typical real-world cases (sometimes called 'medical Newcomb cases') is to rule out cases involving supernatural predictors, time travel, or quantum effects.[37]

---

[36] See Section 5.2 for a response used by fork asymmetry accounts.

[37] Unrealistic cases include those where a predictor *cannot* be outsmarted by considering the basis on which the predictor makes their prediction and using this information to decide some other way. Supernatural means is one way to achieve such reliability. Price defends evidential decision theory *tout court*, even for unrealistic cases. Traditional Newcomb cases (Nozick, 1969) may

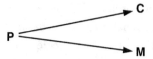

Figure 3 Causal graph showing a pre-migraine state (**P**) as a common cause of chocolate eating (**C**) and migraine (**M**).

Consider the following case (Figure 3). Chloe has noticed a correlation between her eating chocolate and later getting a migraine. She knows this correlation is not due to chocolate *causing* her migraine. Instead, there is a pre-migraine state that causes both her chocolate eating and her migraine. Will evidential decision theory recommend *incorrectly* that Chloe should avoid eating chocolate to avoid a migraine and that she should act now in order to *avoid* the pre-migraine state? If evidential decision theory delivers this result, agency accounts of causation will imply, incorrectly, that there is backwards causation in real-world cases.

Price responds as follows. If Chloe decides to avoid eating chocolate *because* she thinks not eating chocolate is evidence of her not being in the pre-migraine state, this evidential reasoning provides a competing *causal explanation* for why she decides not to eat chocolate. This evidential reasoning *undermines* the correlation that would otherwise obtain between her eating chocolate and the pre-migraine state. Therefore, her decision not to eat the chocolate is no longer good evidence for her not being in the pre-migraine state and Chloe loses her evidential grounds for making that decision. A decision not to eat the chocolate on this basis is 'unstable'. Price argues that evidential decision theory should require us to reach equilibrium judgements, where the evidential relevance of our decision is not undermined by a judgement that we make on its basis. The only stable positions are where the agent either takes her decision to be probabilistically irrelevant to past states or suspends judgement (Price, 1986: 201).

Price (1991, 1992b, 2012) (see also Menzies and Price, 1993) sometimes puts this argument in terms of the agent's assumptions about freedom. If Chloe takes herself to be a free agent in Price's sense (Section 4.1), she considers that she can bring about events in a free and immediate way as the result of deliberation. Chloe knows that her freely deciding to avoid chocolate will *interrupt* the correlation that would otherwise obtain between her decision and the pre-migraine state. Her avoiding the chocolate will therefore not raise the

---

count as unrealistic or contradictory, depending on how they are defined. For discussions, see Price (1986: 208, 1991: 167–8, 2012). Price (1984, 1996: Ch. 8) accepts backwards causation in quantum mechanics.

probability of her not being in the pre-migraine state. Therefore, given that Chloe is aware of these causal facts, evidential decision theory will not recommend that Chloe avoids the chocolate to avoid the pre-migraine state.

If either of these results holds more generally, it seems that agents will not take their freely chosen options now, **A**, to raise the probability of past outcomes, **B**, even when those past outcomes are usually correlated with **A**. Therefore, agents won't take there to be causal relations directed towards the past in our world.

According to Price, evidential correlations towards the past, but not the future, are undermined by free or evidentially stable deliberation. The reason for this asymmetry in undermining is that agents are situated asymmetrically in time (Price, 1992a, 1992b), in the sense that they deliberate before acting (Price, 2007; Price and Weslake, 2009). Because they deliberate before acting, correlations to earlier events are broken by deliberation, while correlations to later events are not.

While our temporal orientation as agents may ultimately be due to thermodynamic or entropic asymmetry, Price argues that the temporal asymmetry of *causation* does not depend on any such physical asymmetry (Price, 1992a: 516, 1992b: 263–5, 2007: 265, 270; Price and Weslake, 2009: 436). Instead, Price claims that causation's temporal asymmetry is perspectival: it is an asymmetry that only holds from our perspective (Price, 1991, 1992a, 1992b, 2007). Were our deliberative perspective to be temporally reversed, such that we acted before deliberating, causation would be temporally reversed as well. The temporal asymmetry of causation 'is a product of an asymmetric viewpoint on a symmetric state of affairs' (Price and Weslake, 2009: 419). However, because we're unaware of this dependence, we *project* onto the world relations that are partly determined by our own contingent perspectives and take causation to be an objective feature of the world (Price, 1991: 173, 2007: 254). We also project our temporally asymmetric orientation as deliberators into situations that lack thermodynamic asymmetries – accounting for our conviction that the temporal asymmetry of causation holds generally.

4.4 Objections to Price's Explanation

There are two immediate concerns with Price's explanation. First, some have worried that Price's account of causation is too anthropocentric (Earman, 1976: 22–3; Hausman, 1997; Field, 2003; Woodward, 2003: 118 ff.). It might seem that Price's explanation of the temporal asymmetry of causation will inherit this worrying anthropocentricity. Second, some have worried that Price's account of causation is circular (Hausman, 1997; Woodward, 2003: 123 ff.). It might seem that Price's explanation will inherit this circularity. I'll begin with the circularity worry.

Price's explanation makes use of causal concepts. One crucial point at which it does is by assuming that the agent takes her evidential or free deliberation to provide a competing '*causal* explanation' for why she decides and acts as she does – one that interrupts the causal relation that would otherwise obtain between the direct option and its usual causes (Price, 1991: 166, my emphasis; see also Price, 1986: 201–2, 208, 1991: 165, 170–1, 1992b: 261, 2007: 281–2; Menzies and Price, 1993: 191). Price is explicit that it is by virtue of the 'causal role [of the judgement] that the judgement [of there being a correlation] is self-defeating' (Price, 1986: 201; see also Price, 2007: 282). The agent must assume that her act is caused by her deliberation and make assumptions about what the usual causes of her action are, for it is those relations that are undermined by deliberation.

When Price first presents the argument that correlations to the past will be undermined (Price, 1986), it is in the context of defending evidential decision theory. In this context, it is no concern if the agent makes causal assumptions. Nor are causal assumptions problematic if the aim is to rule out spurious correlations as causal (Price, 1991, 1992b) or to explain how we come to reason in causal terms or express causal judgements (Price, 1991: 160, 172–3, 2017: 77–8; see also Hitchcock, 1996). However, causal assumptions are a significant concern if the aim is to explain the temporal asymmetry of causation.

Recall that Price aims to explain why agents take causal relations in typical real-world cases to all be directed towards the future. The reason why agents don't take there to be causal relations directed towards the past is because probabilistic correlations towards the past don't survive the assumption of evidential deliberation or free agency. The reason why correlations to the past but not to the future are undermined by deliberation is because (a) free/evidential deliberation severs a direct option from its *usual causes*, (b) the *usual causes* of direct options are always *earlier* events and never later events, and (c) correlations between direct options now and past events are always due to the past event *causing* the direct option (or being a joint effect of a common cause), rather than the direct option causing the past event. Without (b), there is no reason to think that deliberation will break correlations between direct options and past events, rather than between direct options and future events. Without (c), there is no reason to think that *all* correlations between direct options and past events will be undermined by free/evidential deliberation.

However, if the agent assumes (b) and (c), the agent assumes the very temporal asymmetry of causation that was to be explained. Price's agent assumes that direct options are always caused by, but never causes of, correlated past events, implying that effects of direct options lie in the future and that causes of direct options lie in the past.[38] Given that the aim was to explain why agents take there to be a temporal asymmetry of causal relations concerning direct options and other events, Price's explanation is viciously circular – it assumes, as a premise, its own conclusion. Modelling free agency in causal terms, (a), makes this problem unavoidable – one will have to use temporal features of *causation* to explain why free deliberation undermines correlations in one temporal direction and not the other.

Price is aware that his account of *causation* is apt to look circular. He has two responses. The first, on which he puts less weight (Menzies and Price, 1993: 194), is that a circular analysis can still be informative – in the same way that interventionist accounts of causation (Pearl, 2000; Woodward, 2003), which use causal notions, can still be informative. Price's second response is that we have 'direct experience' of agency (1991: 173) and of 'doing one thing and thence achieving another' (Menzies and Price, 1993: 194–5; see also Price, 2017: 76–7), so that the relevant agential concepts can be introduced by ostension. These responses may be enough to show that Price's account of causation is informative and contentful. However, they don't address the circularity in Price's explanation of the temporal asymmetry of causation.

Price's explanation is meant to show why deliberators, characterised 'in a non-causal, epistemic fashion' (Price and Weslake, 2009: 439) and embedded in an environment 'in which causation is not part of the pre-existing furniture' (Price, 2007: 289), come to model the world in temporally asymmetric causal terms. However, the argument that Price gives for why correlations towards the past but not the future are undermined from the agent's point of view requires the agent to *already* model the world in explicitly causal terms. At this point it doesn't matter if circular accounts can be informative or if agential concepts can be introduced by ostension – we have no explanation for even an apparent temporal asymmetry of causation that doesn't assume an apparent temporal asymmetry of causation.

A consequence of this circularity is that, despite Price's claims to trace the temporal asymmetry of causation back to a temporal orientation of deliberation (Price, 1992b: 261–2; see also Price, 1992a: 513; Price and Weslake, 2009: 419), the temporal orientation of deliberation plays no role in Price's explanation. Price claims that the temporal asymmetry of causation 'is a product of an

---

[38] For simplicity, I leave out the possibility that correlated past events may also be joint effects of a common cause. Removing this simplification won't help Price. If Price is to rule out spurious correlations as causal, he must also assume that the common causes of these joint effects lie in the past.

asymmetric viewpoint on a symmetric state of affairs' (Price and Weslake, 2009: 419). Whether we think of **A** as causing a later **B** or **B** as causing an earlier **A** is meant to depend on the temporal orientation of deliberation, such that creatures with the opposite temporal orientation would disagree with us about the temporal direction of causation (Price, 1996: Ch. 7, 2007, 2017). However, the temporal orientation of deliberation does no work in Price's explanation. All the work is done by the fact that deliberation severs direct options from what are taken to be its usual causes – and that those usual causes lie in the past. It doesn't matter if deliberation is in the past or future of direct options. Since the temporal orientation of deliberation is irrelevant to explaining the (apparent) temporal asymmetry of causation, causation turns out not to be perspectival, *even under Price's own account.*[39]

Having seen how serious the circularity worry is, we are in a better position to consider whether Price can give a suitably objective account of the temporal asymmetry of causation. Price's explanation for why agents take causes to come before their effects comes down to the fact that agents take their free deliberation to cause their direct options and they take the usual causes of their direct options to lie in the past. However, Price has no explanation for why agents take the usual causes of their direct options to lie in the past. The apparent temporal asymmetry of causation comes down to beliefs on the part of the agent that we have no explanation for. Therefore, even if we 'translate' Price's explanation into more objective terms, and replace subjective probabilities with objective worldly probabilities, or justify the use of subjective probabilities using a shared agential perspective (Menzies and Price, 1993; Evans, 2020), the circularity problem remains, implying that the account can't be used to trace causal asymmetry back to non-causal physical features of the world or us.

4.5 The Tickle-Defence Explanation

Price's explanation is circular because it models deliberation in causal terms. An obvious alternative is to model deliberation in non-causal terms. One might then explain, in non-causal terms, why correlations to the past are undermined by deliberation. Such an account could plausibly be used to explain the temporal asymmetry of causation. Blanchard (2014) and Fernandes (2017) attempt non-causal explanations of this form using a non-causal defence of evidential decision theory: the so-called tickle defence, a term coined by Lewis (1981a).[40]

---

[39] For other concerns with Price's perspectivalism, see Blanchard (2016: 261–2) and Ismael (2016).

[40] The tickle defence is considered by Nozick (1969) and appealed to by Eells (1982), Horgan (1981), Jeffrey (1981), and Horwich (1987: Ch. 11). For concerns, see Skyrms (1980), Lewis (1981a), Jackson and Pargetter (1983), Sobel (1994), Papineau (2001), and Joyce (2007).

Recall Chloe, deliberating about whether to eat chocolate (see Figure 3). She knows there is a correlation between eating chocolate and migraines because a particular pre-migraine state is a common cause of both. Chloe would like to eat chocolate but is much more concerned with avoiding migraines. According to the tickle defence, if Chloe takes into account all of her evidence, evidential decision theory will *not* recommend she avoid eating chocolate. Evidential decision theory would only recommend she avoid chocolate if doing so would raise the probability of her not being in the pre-migraine state, where the relevant probabilities are those conditional on Chloe's total evidence. However, if Chloe already has evidence that settles her being in the pre-migraine state, avoiding chocolate will not raise the probability of that state, conditional on her total evidence – so avoiding chocolate will not be recommended. Even if Chloe's evidence does not settle her being in the pre-migraine state, provided her evidence provides as much evidence about her pre-migraine state as her chocolate eating does, evidential decision theory will not recommend that she avoid eating chocolate.

Crucial to the tickle defence is the claim that Chloe has evidence of being in the pre-migraine state as she deliberates. More generally, the tickle defence claims that agents always have evidence, as they deliberate, of past states that are correlated with their later actions and decisions. Chloe, for example, will have a desire, urge, or hankering for chocolate (a 'tickle') whenever her later chocolate eating is correlated with her pre-migraine state. Chloe's belief that she has this desire and her belief in the desire's correlation with the pre-migraine state form part of her total evidence and together give her (subjective) evidence that she was in the pre-migraine state. This evidence is independent of what decision she makes now and so it 'screens off' the evidential relevance of her decision and act for the past state. No matter what she decides at this point, she shouldn't take her eating chocolate to be correlated with the pre-migraine state. Evidential decision theorists attempt to show that when there are past states probabilistically correlated with future acts and decisions, these always go via the agent's having evidence of that past state at times in between – evidence that screens off the probabilistic relevance of future acts or decisions for the past state.

If one adopts an agency account of causation, the tickle defence also implies that there will be no causal relations to the past in real-world cases. Backwards causation is implied only if an agent's decision or action now raises the probability of the past state, conditional on her total evidence. However, if an agent has evidence of the past state, then the decision or action does not raise the probability of the past state, conditional on her total evidence. Therefore, causal relations towards the past are never implied. However, this is not so towards the future. Except in the case of spurious correlations, we don't expect an agent's evidence while deliberating to screen off the probabilistic relevance of her decision or action for states in the future. Therefore, there can still be probabilistic correlations between decisions and future states, conditional on the agent's total evidence – implying that there can be forwards causation. Putting these two pieces together, the temporal asymmetry of causation is due to the fact that an agent's evidence while deliberating screens off probabilistic correlations towards the past but not the future.

One way of explaining this asymmetry in screening off is to appeal to temporal features of deliberation. It seems that the source of the agent's evidence in past states are her 'deliberative states' – states such as beliefs, desires, and urges that can serve as part of or inputs to her deliberation. It seems that probabilistic correlations between an agent's decisions and actions now and past states are always 'mediated' by her being in particular deliberative states at times in between – the correlation between the action and the past state only obtains when the deliberative state does (Figure 4). If the agent has the relevant belief that she is in such a deliberative state (and believes in its correlation to the past state) the past-directed correlation will be screened off. However, correlations between decisions and actions now and states in the future are not mediated by deliberative states. Therefore, an agent's total evidence while deliberating screens off probabilistic correlations towards the past but not the future.

This tickle defence explanation is compatible with the requirements that causal relations must be *robust* (Section 3.6) – they must be those that can be employed for a variety of reasons (Albert, 2015: 49–50) or that still hold when one attempts to use them for gain (Fernandes, 2023). By requiring causal correlations to be robust, they must hold when any particular deliberative state is present or absent. Given the response outlined earlier, the correlation only obtains when a particular deliberative state is present. In this way, the robustness response can be put non-causally – avoiding the circularity concern raised against Price's account.

4.6 Evaluating the Tickle-Defence Explanation

There are several kinds of concerns that may be raised against the tickle-defence explanation. The first kind are about the use of the tickle defence in general. The second kind are about whether the explanation traces the temporal asymmetry of causation back to sufficiently fundamental features of the physical world. The third kind concern whether the explanation can recover a suitably general temporal asymmetry of causation. We'll consider each in turn.

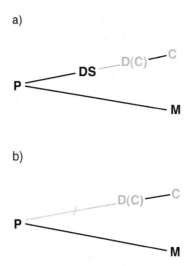

Figure 4 The evidence Chloe has while deliberating on eating chocolate (**C**) for the sake of not being in the pre-migraine state (**P**), given the causal structure in Figure 3. Black indicates states and correlations that Chloe has evidence of. Grey indicates states and correlations that Chloe lacks evidence of. Solid lines indicate evidential correlations. Crossed lines indicate a lack of evidential correlation. (a) Deliberation with a particular deliberative state (**DS**) present. Chloe has evidence of being in a deliberative state that provides evidence of whether she has the pre-migraine state and will get a migraine (**M**), even though it does not settle her decision to eat the chocolate (**D(C)**) or eating chocolate (**C**). Because her decision does not raise the probability of a migraine, given Chloe's total evidence, her eating chocolate does not count as a cause of migraine. (b) Deliberation with a particular deliberative state absent. Because Chloe is never in a particular deliberative state, her decision (**D(C)**) isn't correlated with the pre-migraine state (**P**). Because there is no evidential correlation between her decision and the migraine, her eating chocolate does not count as a cause of migraine.

Debate continues as to whether the tickle defence is adequate as a defence of evidential decision theory (Elliott, 2019; Ahmed, 2021). However, not all objections raised against the tickle defence in that context are relevant to whether it can be used to explain the temporal asymmetry of causation. I'll briefly discuss three objections that are relevant.

First, it may seem that decision theory should issue recommendations not just relative to an agent's own beliefs but relative to *another* agent's beliefs (Jackson and Pargetter, 1983). The tickle defence only explains why the correlation is screened off for Chloe, not for an observer who lacks evidence of Chloe's deliberative states. In response, note that it is no mark against an agent-based explanation if screening off doesn't occur for agents who lack knowledge of Chloe's deliberative states, since a lack of screening off in those cases doesn't imply backwards causation. One might then worry that causal relations shouldn't hold merely from Chloe's perspective. However, note that screening off *can* occur for an observer, provided they have the relevant evidence. While evidential decision theory uses subjective probabilities, screening off can also occur if one uses objective worldly probabilities – provided they are conditional on the same information. Causal relations are particularly relevant for the deliberating agent. However, they are not merely relations that hold from her perspective – they are relations that others can observe and use.

Second, Skyrms (1980: 131) and Lewis (1981a: 10–11) argue that the tickle defence requires agents to have too much self-knowledge. Actual agents may not have credences in the relevant deliberative state or they may not recognise the significance of these states. Chloe may have a desire for chocolate but may not recognise it as evidence of her pre-migraine state. If so, the evidential correlation towards the past will not be screened off.

A possible response is to adopt a less demanding notion of evidence, such that the agent's being *in* a particular deliberative state provides evidence of the past state, even if the agent fails to recognise it as evidence. Even if Chloe doesn't recognise the significance of her desire, the fact that it is objectively correlated with her being in the pre-migraine state implies that Chloe has evidence of the pre-migraine state. Provided that deliberative states are directly accessible to agents, and are objectively correlated with the relevant past states, the deliberative states screen off the correlation.

A second compatible response is that whether screening off occurs depends on how actively the agent is engaged in her deliberation. If she sits back, as it were, and simply lets her deliberation issue with an outcome, her decision to avoid chocolate may well raise the probability of her not being in the pre-migraine state. Screening off occurs only when an agent is suitably reflective and takes into account the relevance of her deliberative states. Causal relations might be those evidential relations that hold conditional on the evidence of suitably reflective deliberating agents.

A further worry arises, however, whichever response one adopts. The notion of evidence should not be so permissive (or the requirements on being reflective so demanding) that agents always have evidence of their decisions and correlated future states while deliberating. Here are two versions of this objection. First, it might seem that, if agents are aware of their beliefs and desires while deliberating, they will always have evidence that settles their decision. This would mean that, conditional on their evidence while deliberating, their decisions would not raise the probability of future states. Second, there are states following deliberation, such as memories, that provide evidence of the decision. These will also screen off the relevance of the decision, if agents have evidence of them while deliberating (my thanks to a reviewer for this point).

One response to the second version is to appeal to an epistemic asymmetry: the fact that we have records of the past and not the future (discussed in the following and in Section 3.3). Given this asymmetry, we may count as having evidence of recent past, but not future, states of ourselves. A second response (to both versions) is to note that the objection generalises to any account of causation that appeals to the effective strategies role. If an account of causation is justified by the fact that causes raise the probability of their effects, for appropriately deliberating agents, there needs to be some appropriate specification of the agent's evidence conditional on which that claim turns out to be true. However, while the objection generalises, it is more severe for agency accounts. In defence of other accounts, one can appeal to causal notions to offer an appropriate specification of the agent's evidence. This is not so if one is using an agency account to explain the temporal asymmetry of causation. For further possible responses, see Fernandes (2017: 703). Altogether, an appropriate specification of the agent's evidence remains an outstanding challenge for agency accounts.

A second kind of concern with the tickle-defence explanation is whether it traces the temporal asymmetry of causation back to sufficiently fundamental features of the physical world. According to the explanation, the temporal asymmetry of causation is due to the fact that correlations between decisions and past states are mediated by deliberative states, while correlations towards future states are not. It might be tempting to think that this asymmetry of mediation is due to facts about *deliberation* alone – the fact that we deliberate before we decide – making the explanation of the temporal asymmetry of causation anthropocentric. However, the asymmetry of meditation is due to worldly structure as well. If worldly probabilistic structure were different, there could be correlations between decisions and past states that weren't mediated by the agent being in a particular state at times in between. In such cases, there would be backwards causation.

For similar reasons, the tickle-defence explanation is not committed to causation being 'perspectival', in the sense that reversing the order of deliberation *alone* would reverse the order of causation. What happens in any 'reversal' of deliberation depends on what happens to the probabilistic structure of the world. In our world, the sequence of correlations between inputs to deliberation, decision, and action is *linear*, in the sense that states at times in between mediate states they are adjacent to. However, this is not just a feature of deliberation – it is a feature of correlations more generally across space-time.

It may be beyond the remit of agency accounts to explain worldly probabilistic structure – it may be a given from which the temporal asymmetry of causation is derived. However, some attempt might be made to explain the temporal asymmetry of deliberation: the fact that we deliberate before we decide. One simple explanation begins by characterising deliberation as an information-gathering process – agents gather information from earlier states of the world and themselves and store this in the form of deliberative states. A general feature of recording systems in our world is that they gather information from the past and retain it towards the future, rather than the reverse (Reichenbach, 1956; Albert, 2000: Ch. 6; Fernandes, 2022b). However, while this might explain why *deliberation* is temporally asymmetric, it doesn't explain why deliberation comes prior to decision – why decision temporally concludes deliberation.

Expanding on this first attempt, one might require decisions to be appropriately sensitive to information gathered during deliberation. As a fact about our world, it seems that decisions are insensitive to information gathered *after* the decision – what you learn tomorrow is not appropriately correlated with the decisions you made yesterday. Therefore, information gathered after your decision is not part of deliberation: it doesn't play the right functional role. This asymmetry appears to also be an instance of a more general temporal asymmetry of recording devices – the inputs that are relevant for outputs must be prior in time to their outputs. The temporal asymmetry of recording devices might itself be explained in broadly entropic terms (see, for example, Reichenbach, 1956; Albert, 2000; Fernandes, 2022b).[41]

Given very general features of deliberation and the probabilistic structure of the world, there is only one way that deliberation could have been temporally oriented. Therefore, it will be hard to make sense of counterfactuals where one reverses the direction of deliberation but keeps probabilistic structure intact – the kind of counterfactuals that Price appeals to (Section 4.4). These agent-based explanations have more in common with statistical mechanical accounts than Price's account regarding how closely they relate the temporal asymmetry of causation to physical temporal asymmetries. Using an 'objective' agency explanation, the temporal asymmetry of causation is ultimately due to whatever physical temporal asymmetries explain the temporal asymmetry of recording devices combined with general temporally symmetric features of agency and

---

[41] For an alternative account of why deliberation is temporally asymmetric, see Fernandes (2017). Ismael (2016: 260–1) and Price (2007: 275–8) also suggest that epistemic constraints will be relevant to explaining temporal features of deliberation, without specifying how.

general features of worldly structure – the latter of which may themselves relate to the entropic structure of the universe.

A third kind of concern raised against agent-based explanations is whether they give a sufficiently *general* account of the temporal asymmetry of causation – one that can explain causal asymmetry in cases where agents can't deliberate. For related concerns, see Hausman (1997) and Woodward (2016).

Standard methods for extending agency accounts to cases where agents can't deliberate rely on identifying structural similarities between set-ups where agents can deliberate and those where they can't (Menzies and Price, 1993: 197–8; Fernandes, 2017: 698–700; Price, 2017: 88–90). Appeals to structural similarities can be made even if one does not reduce causation to physical structure. One may instead use these similarities to evaluate counterfactuals about what probabilistic relations would obtain, were an agent to deliberate. For simplicity, however, I'll consider how structural similarities can be used to defend a reductive account. According to the kind of reductive account discussed above (Section 4.2), causal relations are objective worldly probabilities of the kind useful to deliberating agents. In cases where agents can deliberate, causal relations are probabilistic relations that agents *can* use to achieve the outcomes they seek. However, the same kind of probabilistic relations can obtain in settings where agents can't deliberate on the relevant outcome (such as on the eruption of a volcano) or can't exist (such as inside the sun). These relations will count as causal because they are probabilistic relations of the same *kind*, sharing similar structural features, as those found in situations where agents can deliberate.

One crucial feature of the probabilistic relations that such an account will identify as causal will be their temporal asymmetry – only probabilistic relations that are temporally asymmetric will be potentially useful to deliberating agents in our world. Deliberating agents can only make use of correlations towards the future, given the norms of deliberation and given general features of the probabilistic structure of our world. Given that agents satisfy these norms (and given the background probabilistic structure), agents effectively function as 'intervention devices' that break probabilistic correlations immediately before the putative cause but not after. Therefore, even in situations where agents can't deliberate, the probabilistic relations that the agency account will identify as causal will all be future directed in our world. What about in situations lacking probabilistic (or entropic) asymmetry? As with statistical mechanical accounts (Section 3.5), one might deny there is a temporal asymmetry of causation (or causation at all) in these settings or invoke a projectivist component and take the probabilistic asymmetry that obtains around us to be projected into these new settings. My preference is to allow causation but deny the temporal asymmetry of causation in these settings; however, I suspect that our causal concept and the function of causation are not sufficiently determinate to settle which of these responses we should adopt.

I've suggested that agency explanations of the temporal asymmetry of causation are defensible, provided they can give a non-causal explanation of why correlations to the past (but not the future) are undermined by deliberation. I've also suggested that the most satisfactory explanation seeks to explain the asymmetry of undermining by appeal to physical asymmetries, as well as features of agents. Having seen how far agency accounts may rely on physical asymmetries, it is time to compare agency accounts and statistical mechanical accounts.

5 Future Directions

In this final section, I consider prospects for reconciling agency and statistical mechanical accounts (Section 5.1), before examining fork asymmetry accounts and whether they can be reconciled with statistical mechanical and agency accounts (Section 5.2). The Element ends with a summary of the state of these three programmes (Section 5.3).

5.1 Reconciling Statistical Mechanical and Agency Accounts

Statistical mechanical and agency-based explanations of the temporal asymmetry of causation have important features in common. Given these similarities, can these accounts be reconciled? If so, what kind of reconciliation is to be preferred?

As noted previously (Section 4.6), both agent-based and statistical mechanical explanations ultimately trace the temporal asymmetry of causation back to physical asymmetries related to entropy. Reductive agency accounts may also agree with statistical mechanical accounts on identifying causal relations as objective probabilities. Plausibly, agency and statistical mechanical accounts will also identify the same relations as causal, insofar as they adopt the same probabilistic structure and use the same agency resources to rule out backwards causation. The major difference between these accounts is the *form* of their explanations for the temporal asymmetry of causation.

According to statistical mechanical accounts, the major work required to explain the temporal asymmetry of causation is to identify a temporal asymmetry in probabilistic structure that, combined with a temporally neutral way of evaluating counterfactuals, delivers a 'for the most part' temporal asymmetry of counterfactual dependence. In pursuit of this aim, Albert's and Loewer's statistical mechanical accounts use counterfactuals evaluated by holding parts of the present fixed, even when an agent has no evidence of those parts (unlike agency accounts).

Considerations of agency are only introduced to deal with exceptions to counterfactual asymmetry. Moreover, the justification for the method of evaluating counterfactuals is a secondary affair – the focus is on delivering temporal asymmetry.

By contrast, agent-based explanations focus from the start on identifying probabilistic structure that is *relevant* to deliberating agents. Those defending agent-based explanations argue that satisfying this constraint will imply a temporally asymmetry in the probabilities, such that the reason why the probabilities (and thus causation) turn out to be asymmetric depends in part on features of agents. Even if the probabilities themselves are temporally asymmetric before agential considerations are introduced, that asymmetry by itself does not explain the temporal asymmetry of causation. Rather than agency being a means of dealing with counterexamples, and justification being a secondary affair, the *need* for causal relations to be temporally asymmetric accounts for why they turn out to be so (given that the required probabilistic structure exists). By requiring causal relations to be useful, agency accounts aim to do away with the transition period entirely (assuming that the concern raised in Section 4.3 is dealt with). Because correlations during that period can't be made use of, they don't appear in our 'causal map' of the universe. There is no need to invoke a way of evaluating counterfactuals that merely minimises the transition period.

My own preference is for an agent-based explanation. Here are three reasons. First, as previously mentioned (Section 3.7), the statistical mechanical explanation can't explain a strict temporal asymmetry of causation without introducing features of agents. However, once features of agents are introduced to rule out backwards influence, these same features can be used to derive a strict causal asymmetry from the start, without going via a rough asymmetry first (Fernandes, 2016b: 203–18; Loew, 2017).

Second, because the statistical mechanical explanation requires counterfactuals as a 'half-way step', defenders get engaged in disputes over how to evaluate counterfactuals that are *avoidable* in this context. These avoidable disputes include how the recipe for evaluating counterfactuals should balance the cost of miracles (or other surprising dynamics) against the cost of admitting backwards counterfactual dependence (Sections 3.2 and 3.6) and how the recipe should treat chancy events that we don't control and that have no implications for what we control – the issue of 'hindsight' (Maudlin, 2007: Ch. 1).

Third, agency accounts may be more generalisable to worlds that lack that thermodynamic asymmetry – such as worlds involving macroscopic backwards causation or time travel. Agency accounts use a local probabilistic structure of a kind that is accessible to agents. In situations involving backwards causation, evaluating counterfactuals using local structure may yield better results than using global structure like statistical mechanical accounts do (see Fernandes, 2021, 2022a).

That said, I suspect one's preference between these accounts will be largely determined by what one wants an account of causation primarily to *achieve*: either the task of *identification* (stating *what* relations get picked out as causal in our world) or the task of *justification* (explaining *why* those relations should be picked out as causal). These tasks aren't incompatible. However, they motivate different approaches to explaining the temporal asymmetry of causation.[42]

5.2 Fork Asymmetry Accounts

While statistical mechanical and agency-based explanations of the temporal asymmetry of causation have received more recent attention, there are other approaches to causation that might be used to explain the temporal asymmetry of causation – so-called fork asymmetry accounts.

Fork asymmetry accounts take causal relations to imply certain patterns in macro-probabilistic structure – probabilities concerning (typically types of) macrostates or macro events (Reichenbach, 1956; Hausman, 1982, 1998; Papineau, 1985, 1992; Horwich, 1987; Arntzenius, 1990; Dowe, 2000: Ch. 8).[43] Insofar as these patterns appear in one temporal direction and not the other, it seems that these patterns may explain the temporal asymmetry of causation – particularly if causal relations are identified with these patterns (Papineau, 1992). However, even if one takes causal relations to merely *imply* patterns in macro probabilities, one may still be able to explain the temporal asymmetry of causation.

Consider interventionist accounts (Cartwright, 1979; Papineau, 1985; Spirtes, Glymour, and Scheines, 1993; Pearl, 2000; Woodward, 2003, 2007; Hitchcock, 2007). Interventionist accounts take the existence of causal relations to imply that the correlation between cause and effect will be somewhat stable when the cause is intervened in by a suitable causal process. While interventionists don't typically aim to explain the temporal asymmetry of causation, often instead taking it to be a useful heuristic for discovering causal relations,

---

[42] See Dieks (1986) for a different but related reconciliation between physicalist and agent-based accounts.

[43] One might take these macro probabilities to derive from probabilities concerning microstates or to derive more directly from statistical regularities and other patterns in macroscopic events. As with statistical mechanical and agency accounts, it is important that the probabilities are well defined towards the causal and temporal past.

Papineau (1985) and Field (2003) have suggested that an asymmetry in the relevant macro-probabilistic structure may explain the temporal asymmetry of causation, even if causal relations do not reduce to that structure.[44]

To see how a fork asymmetry account might explain the temporal asymmetry of causation, consider Reichenbach's approach. Reichenbach (1956: Section 19) introduces a screening off condition that relates causal relations to probabilities. Such a condition appears in an altered form in interventionist accounts, where it becomes known as the causal Markov condition (for discussion, see Field, 2003; Weslake, 2006). Say two event (or state) types are correlated: the spouting of fountain A (**A**) and fountain B (**B**). **A** and **B** occur simultaneously more often than would be expected by mere coincidence; the probability of **A**+**B** (the co-occurrence of **A** and **B** within a time frame) is greater than the product of their independent probabilities (of occurring within that time frame):

$$P(A\&B) > P(A).P(B) \tag{1}$$

Reichenbach suggests that when event types **A** and **B** are correlated and occur simultaneously, there will be an event type **C** that is positively correlated with **A** and **B** and that 'screens off' the probabilistic relevance of **A** and **B** for each other. In other words, **A** and **B** are no longer correlated once **C** is conditionalised on. A certain water flow in the chamber beneath, **C**, may be positively correlated with each fountain spouting, but, once you conditionalise on **C**, **A** and **B** appear probabilistically independent of one another. **C** will satisfy the following relations:

$$P(A|C) > P(A|\neg C) \tag{2}$$

$$P(B|C) > P(B|\neg C) \tag{3}$$

$$P(A\&B|C) = P(A|C).P(B|C) \tag{4}$$

$$P(A\&B|\neg C) = P(A|\neg C).P(B|\neg C) \tag{5}$$

These probabilistic relations can be represented using a fork structure (Figure 5).

Reichenbach claims that correlated event types **A** and **B** occurring simultaneously will always be screened off by an *earlier* event type **C** (their common cause) comprising a fork directed towards the future. While **A** and **B** may

---

[44] It might seem that interventionist accounts directly explain the direction of causation, since interventions come from the past and therefore interrupt correlations towards the past. For concerns with that proposal, see Weslake (2006) and Section 4.4.

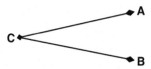

Figure 5 Correlational graph showing an event type **C** screening off the
correlation between **A** and **B**.

sometimes be screened off by a later event type **D** (what we come to call a joint
effect), comprising a fork directed towards the past, screening off by later events
only happens when there is also screening off by earlier events. There are no
'open' forks towards the past, whereas there are open forks towards the future.
Since open forks are always directed towards the future, (common) causes
always come prior in time to their effects.

Some work will be required to show that fork asymmetry can derive a strict
causal asymmetry in our world.[45] For example, since there must be a macro-
probabilistic structure to derive a temporal asymmetry of causation, it will be
difficult to derive causal asymmetry at the micro level or in worlds or parts of
our world lacking asymmetries in macro-probabilistic structure (Price, 1992a,
1992b). However, given that causation appears to be primarily a macroscopic
phenomenon (Section 2.4), one might simply deny that there is causation in
these settings (Papineau, 1992; Field, 2003).

Assuming such concerns can be answered, one might stop the explanation at
this point and simply take it to be a contingent empirical fact of our world that
there is an asymmetry in macro-probabilistic structure – an asymmetry that
implies a temporal asymmetry of causation. However, a more satisfying explanation will also account for *why* the world exhibits temporal asymmetry in its
probabilistic structure. A promising approach is to appeal to an asymmetry in
the boundary conditions of the universe – that there is randomness (sometimes
called chaos) or statistical independence of variables in initial but not final
conditions (Papineau, 1985; Horwich, 1987: 72–5; Frisch, 2014).[46] The initial
randomness might concern macro variables (Papineau), micro variables
(Horwich), or some combination (Frisch). In its micro-variables formulation,

---

[45] Numerous counterexamples to Reichenbach's principle of common cause have been raised
(Sober, 1988; Arntzenius, 1992; Papineau, 1992; Weslake, 2006), leading to refinements in
screening off conditions (Arntzenius, 1992; Papineau, 1992; Price, 1992b; Dowe, 2000; Pearl,
2000; Woodward, 2003). As with other accounts, fork asymmetry depends on restricting the
relevant variables (see Section 3.4). The need for appropriately restricted variables creates
problems for certain ways of responding to counterexamples. For discussion, see Arntzenius
(1990) and Weslake (2006).

[46] Arntzenius (1992) takes a different but related approach. Frisch (2014: 201) posits both initial
randomness and a primitive temporal asymmetry of causation.

the universe begins in a typical microstate given its initial macrostate (micro randomness), such that correlations between macro variables don't arise in a conspiratorial manner as the universe evolves towards the future. There aren't correlations between macro variables 'hidden' in the initial microstate of the universe; any correlations that appear are the result of causal structure. This assumption is reversed concerning the universe's final state. The universe ends in an *atypical* microstate given its final macrostate (micro order), such that correlations *do* appear conspiratorially as the universe evolves towards the past. This asymmetry in micro randomness produces an asymmetry in probabilistic structure such that correlations towards the past (but not the future) can be attributed to common causes.

An assumption of initial micro randomness is similar to the statistical postulate. However, the fork asymmetry explanation must combine an assumption of initial micro randomness with an assumption of final *micro order*, not just the *lack* of a micro-randomness constraint. Otherwise, the universe may have started out in a high-entropy state, or may end in a micro-random state, and there would be no fork asymmetry. Since micro order in the future implies a low-entropy past, the assumptions of initial micro randomness and final micro order are, taking into account differences in how micro randomness is formulated, equivalent to an assumption of an initial low-entropy condition (similar to the past hypothesis) combined with the statistical postulate (Arntzenius, 1990; Price, 1992b).[47] I have no intuitions to press about which posits are explanatorily more basic. Some have preferred to explain the future by the past (Albert, 2000; Maudlin, 2007: Ch. 4; Loewer, 2012), others explain the macro by the micro (Horwich, 1987: Ch. 4), and others suggest that neither seems satisfactory in this context (Price, 1992b).

Given that fork asymmetry accounts ultimately trace the temporal asymmetry of causation back to similar or equivalent posits to those used by statistical mechanical accounts, are these accounts equivalent? No. For a first example, consider Lewis' (1979) account. Lewis' asymmetry of overdetermination, that is, the fact that events leave multiple traces in their futures but not their pasts (Section 3.1), is an example of fork asymmetry. Traces are correlated with their common cause and with each other, but their correlation with each other is screened off by their common cause. However, Lewis does not identify causation with patterns in macro probabilities. Instead, causal relations reduce to counterfactual relations and the asymmetry of overdetermination is used to argue for a temporal asymmetry of counterfactuals. Similarly, contemporary

---

[47] Fork asymmetry and statistical mechanical accounts both face the issue of how far backwards and forwards in time the relevant posits should be placed. These posits may need to refer to the start and end of whatever entropy curve we are on.

statistical mechanical accounts by Albert and Loewer don't identify causal relations with patterns in macro probabilities. Instead, they reduce causal relations to counterfactuals and use an asymmetry of records to argue that there will be temporal asymmetries of counterfactuals. Counterfactual and fork asymmetry accounts disagree on what causal relations are and what conditions must be met for a causal relation to obtain.

Moreover, statistical mechanical and fork asymmetry accounts may disagree on what causal relations obtain in our world. Albert and Loewer are committed to statistical mechanical probabilities deriving all of the macro-probabilistic structure that there is – including fork asymmetry (Loewer, 2012; Albert, 2015: 57). However, to evaluate counterfactuals, one needs a *recipe*, in addition to probabilities. Not all probabilistic relations count as causal. Under a fork asymmetry approach, one identifies causal structure using a particular pattern in the macro-probabilistic structure, such as open forks. Because statistical mechanical and fork asymmetry accounts use different criteria in addition to probabilities to pick out causal relations, there is no guarantee that they will agree on what causal relations obtain. To take a simple example, if there are cases where an event is only probabilistically correlated with a single later event, as part of the probabilistic structure intrinsic to the system, there is no open fork structure that would allow the first event to be identified as a cause of the second. However, a statistical mechanical account will identify the first as a cause of the second, if the second depends counterfactually on the first.[48]

Reichenbach (1956) suggests one way in which fork asymmetry and statistical mechanical accounts might be connected.[49] While Reichenbach is known for defending a fork asymmetry account, he takes the fork asymmetry to be a special case of a more basic causal asymmetry. This more basic causal asymmetry is derived using a statistical mechanical account that is different from Albert's and Loewer's accounts. According to Reichenbach (1956: Section 18), causes are lower entropy states of entropy-increasing systems that render probable higher entropy states of these systems – which come to be called their effects. These higher entropy states record the lower entropy states and the lower entropy states cause the higher entropy states – making causation the inverse of recording.[50] Because the universe has a local asymmetry of entropy, reflected in the behaviour of individual subsystems, causes will almost always come before their effects.

---

[48] Another potential discrepancy concerns the transition period – see Section 3.6 and Papineau (1992).

[49] For a related approach, see Arntzenius (1990).

[50] Reichenbach reserves the terms 'records' and 'causes' for states of systems characterised macroscopically. However, he takes the same phenomena to appear at the micro level.

Reichenbach (1956: Section 19) takes the fork asymmetry to be a special case of this causal asymmetry. The co-occurrence of **A** and **B**, **A+B**, is an unlikely state. It may, however, be rendered probable by a state type in the past, **C**, which involves the interaction of two individual systems and which is a more unlikely (and therefore a lower entropy) state of the joint system, compared with **A+B**. If so, **C** counts as a cause of **A+B**, using Reichenbach's statistical mechanical definition of cause. Later higher entropy states, what we come to call joint effects, **D**, may indicate **A+B** but do not render **A+B** more probable. **D** is merely a probable product of the joint system's evolution, given **A+B**.[51]

Before we get to problems, note what Reichenbach's explanation would achieve. It would explain how fork asymmetry causal relations are special cases of more general causal relations. It would also explain how asymmetries in both relations are manifestations of an underlying asymmetry in probability (that the universe heads towards more probable states towards the future), which amounts to an entropy gradient of the universe.

Of course, there are things one would want to hear much more about. First, what relations should we identify as causal? It may be that the subset identified using a fork asymmetry account are more appropriately characterised as causal relations, given how we use causal reasoning.

Second, one may be suspicious of particular aspects of Reichenbach's account, such as the way he relates probabilities concerning joint systems and individual systems, and his extension of concepts such as entropy and statistics from the micro level to the macro level (Earman, 1974). Reichenbach is not well placed to address these concerns, since he avoids employing anything like a statistical postulate, making it hard to see how statistics at the micro level give rise to statistics at the macro level or how probabilities concerning different systems relate. However, with the statistical postulate or similar posits in play, there may be a way to reconcile probabilities and concepts of entropy across levels and systems (Loewer, 2012; Albert, 2015: 57; Fernandes, 2022b).

Having considered how fork asymmetry accounts may be reconciled with statistical mechanical accounts, let us consider the relation between fork asymmetry and agency accounts. In principle, defenders of fork asymmetry accounts are interested in agency, as they intend to show that the relations they identify as causal will play the appropriate role for agents (Papineau, 1992; Pearl, 2000: Ch. 4; Woodward, 2003: Ch. 1). Considerations of agency may justify fork asymmetry accounts.

Some work has been done on attempting to unify agency and interventionist accounts (Price, 2017). However, most discussion in this setting assumes that

---

[51] For a related proposal, see Sober and Barrett (1992).

agents are causal interveners without explaining why agents would be so. Sometimes interventions are specified in terms that suggest that they are directly relevant to agents – such as Pearl's (2000: 107–9) 'do' operator. However, little is done to link up these formal definitions with features of agents, except by stipulation. While Woodward (2003: 7) claims interventionist causal relations are relevant for manipulation and control, he unhelpfully specifies manipulation and control using the same interventionist counterfactuals that he uses to specify causal relations (for similar concerns, see Weslake, 2006; Price and Weslake, 2009).

There are attempts to explain why causal relations will be useful to agents, if causal relations reduce to or imply fork asymmetry patterns (Hausman, 1982; Papineau, 1992; Price, 1992b). A key idea is that agents need correlations that are 'robust' in the sense that they hold independently of how the first relatum is brought about. The correlation from cause to effect satisfies this requirement. However, the correlation from effect to cause does not, since the effect is correlated with a given cause only when the effect is brought about by that particular cause. Taking this approach, Papineau (1992) argues that fork asymmetry causal relations are relevant for agents in bringing about desired outcomes because they both (a) are robust and (b) raise the probability of desired outcomes, given an agent's decisions. If an agent's decisions are themselves causes, only correlations from cause to effect will satisfy these requirements.

I argued earlier (Section 4.4) that Price's causal explanation of undermining (what amounts to showing that certain correlations are not robust) was problematic when used as an explanation for the temporal asymmetry of causation, since his explanation presupposed temporally asymmetric causal relations. However, a causal explanation of robustness might be used to *justify* why causal relations are useful to agents, if the temporal asymmetry of causation is explained by other means. Papineau's causal explanation involves some threat of circularity, since it assumes an agent's decisions are causes – and that assumption, independent of further argument, already suggests causal relations will be useful to agents. However, Papineau does more than merely stipulate the usefulness of causation. He uses the assumption that agents' decisions are causes to show how causal relations are uniquely useful correlations for agents. While more could be said to defend the robustness requirement, perhaps by relating it to paradigmatic cases of free agency, Papineau's suggestion is a promising one for unifying fork asymmetry and agency accounts – perhaps the probabilistic relations that agents can make use of will turn out to be just those identified by a fork asymmetry account. Via this route, there may even be a reconciliation between fork asymmetry and statistical mechanical accounts.

5.3 Conclusion

We have examined three empirically based programmes for explaining the temporal asymmetry of causation: statistical mechanical accounts, agency accounts, and fork asymmetry accounts. Each has a distinct starting point. Statistical mechanical accounts reduce causal relations to counterfactuals and are primarily interested in using the resources of statistical mechanics to derive causal relations and their temporal asymmetry. Agency accounts relate causal relations to probabilities of relevance to deliberating agents and are primarily interested in justifying why a given analysis of causation is appropriate; they use features of agents to derive causal relations and their temporal asymmetry. Fork asymmetry accounts relate causal relations to patterns in probabilistic structure concerning macro variables and are primarily interested in deriving causal relations from patterns in probabilistic structure – although some defenders are also interested in how this derivation may explain the temporal asymmetry of causation.

Even though these programmes have distinct starting points, as they have developed they have come to have important features in common. First, while statistical mechanical accounts have traditionally been most focused on relating causal and entropic asymmetries, all programmes can ultimately trace the temporal asymmetry of causation back to combinations of initial and boundary conditions of the universe of the kind that are typically used to explain entropic asymmetry. While their explanations differ, and questions are still to be answered about which posits are more explanatory, all accounts can identify an empirical source of the temporal asymmetry of causation.

Second, while agency accounts have traditionally been the most focused on showing that the role of causation is satisfied by a given account, all programmes can relate causation to the needs of deliberating agents – and so provide an answer to why causation, thus understood, is apt to play a causal role (Section 2.4). While more could be said to explicate the full range of causal roles, and the relevant needs and features of agents, all can provide some role-based justification for their account of causation. For this reason, all can provide a non-trivial account of causation's temporal asymmetry – one that avoids putting in the asymmetry 'by hand' (Section 1.2) or reverse engineering a relation that is temporally asymmetric (Section 3.2).

There are, of course, questions left unanswered. First, it is not clear that all programmes are extensionally equivalent. While I suggested (Section 5.1) that statistical mechanical and agency accounts currently identify the same relations as causal, a similar argument does not hold for fork asymmetry accounts. There are examples, such as Reichenbach's account, where fork asymmetry causes are a subset of statistical mechanical causes. More work is needed to identify whether particular fork asymmetry accounts are equivalent to particular statistical mechanical accounts and which are preferred. Moreover, developments in any of these programmes may affect their relation to agency accounts.

Second, even accounts that are extensionally equivalent offer different explanations of the temporal asymmetry of causation. Once we start deriving temporal asymmetries, there are different candidates to explain causation's temporal asymmetry, particularly concerning the explanation's intermediary steps. Asymmetries in probabilistic structure (such as forks, records, and traces) play a different role in fork asymmetry and statistical mechanical accounts (Section 5.2). Asymmetries of agency play a major role in agency accounts, but only a minor role in statistical mechanical accounts (Section 5.1). It may be that adopting particular accounts of explanation will help adjudicate some of these matters, including whether asymmetries in probabilistic structure can explain causal asymmetry if causal relations don't reduce to probabilities.

Third, the possible metaphysics to accompany these programmes and explanations is currently unsettled. On offer are accounts that reduce causal relations to counterfactual relations and probabilities (Reichenbach, 1956; Papineau, 1992; Albert, 2000: Ch. 6, 2014, 2015: Ch. 2, 2023; Loewer, 2007, 2012; Blanchard, 2014), accounts that treat causal relations as primitive or at least unreduced (Papineau, 1985; Pearl, 2000; Woodward, 2003; Ismael, 2007, 2012, 2013, 2016), and accounts that deny there is a metaphysics of causation to be had at all (Price, 1991, 1992a, 1992b, 1996, 2007, 2012, 2017; Price and Weslake, 2009). While statistical mechanical accounts have traditionally been the most committed to reducing causation, adopting a particular explanation of the temporal asymmetry of causation does not straightforwardly settle the metaphysics of causation.

What I hope is clear, however, is just how fruitful investigating the temporal asymmetry of causation is for making sense of causation and for understanding its place in a physical world. Independently of which of the above explanations we adopt, the business of explaining the temporal asymmetry of causation ties causation to a range of temporal asymmetries, including those relating to probability and entropy, and provides us with a much richer understanding of causation's role in our lives.

References

Ahmed, A. (2021). *Evidential Decision Theory*, Cambridge, UK: Cambridge University Press.

Albert, D. Z. (1992). *Quantum Mechanics and Experience*, Cambridge, MA: Harvard University Press.

(1994). Quantum mechanics and the approach to thermodynamic equilibrium, *British Journal for the Philosophy of Science*, **45**, 669–77.

(2000). *Time and Chance*, Cambridge, MA: Harvard University Press.

(2014). The sharpness of the distinction between past and future, in A. Wilson, ed., *Asymmetries of Chance and Time*, Oxford: Oxford University Press, pp. 160–74.

(2015). *After Physics*, Cambridge, MA: Harvard University Press.

(2023). Conclusion, in B. Loewer, B. Weslake, and E. Winsberg, eds., *The Probability Map of the Universe: Essays on David Albert's Time and Chance*, Cambridge, MA: Harvard University Press, pp. 351–74.

Anscombe, G. E. M. (1975). Causality and determination, in E. Sosa, ed., *Causation and Conditionals*, Oxford: Oxford University Press, pp. 63–81.

Armstrong, D. M. (2004). Going through the open door again: Counterfactual versus singularist theories of causation, in J. Collins, N. Hall, and L. Paul, eds., *Causation and Counterfactuals*, Cambridge, MA: MIT Press, pp. 445–57.

Arntzenius, F. (1990). Physics and common causes, *Synthese*, **82**(1), 77–96.

(1992). The common cause principle, *Proceedings of the Biennial Meeting of the Philosophy of Science Association 1992*, **2**, 227–37.

Arntzenius, F. and Maudlin, T. (2013). Time travel and modern physics, in E. N. Zalta, ed., *The Stanford Encyclopedia of Philosophy*, Winter 2013 Edition, Online Encyclopaedia. https://plato.stanford.edu/archives/win2013/entries/time-travel-phys/.

Barrett, J. (2020). *The Conceptual Foundations of Quantum Mechanics*, Oxford: Oxford University Press.

Beebee, H. (2015). Causation, projection, inference and agency, in R. N. Johnson and M. Smith, eds., *Passions and Projections: Themes from the Philosophy of Simon Blackburn*, New York: Oxford University Press, pp. 25–48.

Bennett, J. (1984). Counterfactuals and temporal direction, *The Philosophical Review*, **93**(1), 57–91.

Blanchard, T. (2014). Causation in a physical world, Ph.D. thesis, Rutgers University.

(2015). Douglas Kutach: Causation and its basis in fundamental physics, *Philosophy of Science*, **82**(2), 330–3.

(2016). Physics and causation, *Philosophy Compass*, **11**(5), 256–66.

Bromberger, S. (1966). Why-questions, in R. G. Colodny, ed., *Mind and Cosmos: Essays in Contemporary Science and Philosophy*, Pittsburgh: University of Pittsburgh Press, pp. 86–111.

Carroll, J. (1994). *Laws of Nature*, Cambridge, UK: Cambridge University Press.

Cartwright, N. (1979). Causal laws and effective strategies. *Noûs*, **13**(4), 419–37.

(1983). *How the Laws of Physics Lie*, Oxford: Clarendon Press.

Collingwood, R. G. (1940). *An Essay on Metaphysics*, Oxford: Clarendon Press.

Dieks, D. (1986). Physics and the direction of causation, *Erkenntnis*, **25**(1), 85–110.

Dorr, C. (2016). Against counterfactual miracles, *Philosophical Review*, **125**(2), 241–86.

Dowe, P. (1992). Process causality and asymmetry, *Erkenntnis*, **37**(2), 179–96.

(2000). *Physical Causation*, New York: Cambridge University Press.

Dummett, M. (1964). Bringing about the past, *The Philosophical Review*, **73**(3), 338–59.

Eagle, A. (2007). Pragmatic causation, in H. Price and R. Corry, eds., *Causation, Physics, and the Constitution of Reality*, Oxford: Oxford University Press, pp. 156–90.

Earman, J. (1974). An attempt to add a little direction to 'the problem of the direction of time', *Philosophy of Science*, **41**(1), 15–47.

(1976). Causation: A matter of life and death, *The Journal of Philosophy*, **73** (1), 5–25.

(1986). *A Primer on Determinism*, Dordrecht: Reidel.

(2006). The 'past hypothesis': Not even false, *Studies in History and Philosophy of Modern Physics*, **37**, 399–430.

Eells, E. (1982). *Rational Decision and Causality*, Cambridge, UK: Cambridge University Press.

Elga, A. (2001). Statistical mechanics and the asymmetry of counterfactual dependence, *Philosophy of Science*, **68**(3), S313–24.

Elliott, E. (2019). Normative decision theory, *Analysis*, **79**(4), 755–72.

Evans, P. (2020). Perspectival objectivity, *European Journal for Philosophy of Science*, **10**(2), 1–21.

Farr, M. and Reutlinger, A. (2013). A relic of a bygone age? Causation, time symmetry and the directionality argument, *Erkenntnis*, **78**(2), 215–35.

Faye, J. (2019). Backward causation, in E. N. Zalta, ed., *The Stanford Encyclopedia of Philosophy*, Spring 2021 Edition, Online Encyclopaedia. https://plato.stanford.edu/archives/spr2021/entries/causation-backwards/.

Fernandes, A. (2016a). Varieties of epistemic freedom, *Australasian Journal of Philosophy*, **94**(4), 736–51.

(2016b). A deliberative account of causation: How the evidence of deliberating agents accounts for causation and its temporal direction, Ph.D. thesis, Columbia University.

(2017). A deliberative approach to causation, *Philosophy and Phenomenological Research*, **95**(3), 686–708.

(2018). Causation, further themes, in *The Routledge Encyclopedia of Philosophy*, Online Encyclopaedia. www.rep.routledge.com/articles/thematic/causation-further-themes/v-2.

(2021). Time travel and counterfactual asymmetry, *Synthese*, **198**(3), 1983–2001.

(2022a). Back to the present: How not to use counterfactuals to explain causal asymmetry, *Philosophies*, **7**(2), 43.

(2022b). How to explain the direction of time, *Synthese*, **200**, 389.

(2023). Time, flies, and why we can't control the past, in B. Loewer, B. Weslake, and E. Winsberg, eds., *The Probability Map of the Universe: Essays on David Albert's Time and Chance*, Cambridge, MA: Harvard University Press, pp. 312–34.

Feynman, R. (1965). *The Character of Physical Law*, Cambridge, MA: MIT Press.

Field, H. (2003). Causation in a physical world, in M. J. Loux and D. W. Zimmerman, eds., *The Oxford Handbook of Metaphysics*, Oxford: Oxford University Press, pp. 435–60.

Friederich, S. and Evans, P. W. (2019). Retrocausality in quantum mechanics, in E. N. Zalta, ed., *The Stanford Encyclopedia of Philosophy*, Summer 2019 Edition, Online Encyclopaedia. https://plato.stanford.edu/archives/sum2019/entries/qm-retrocausality/.

Frisch, M. (2007). Causation, counterfactuals, and the past-hypothesis, in H. Price and R. Corry, eds., *Causation, Physics, and the Constitution of Reality*, Oxford: Oxford University Press, pp. 351–96.

(2010). Does a low-entropy constraint prevent us from influencing the past? in G. Ernst and A. Hüttemann, eds., *Time, Chance and Reduction*, Cambridge, UK: Cambridge University Press, pp. 13–33.

(2012). No place for causes? Causal skepticism in physics, *European Journal for Philosophy of Science*, **2**(3), 313–36.

(2014). *Causal Reasoning in Physics*, Cambridge, UK: Cambridge University Press.

Faye, J. (2021). Backward causation, in E. N. Zalta, ed., *The Stanford Encyclopedia of Philosophy*, Spring 2021 Edition, Online Encyclopaedia. https://plato.stanford.edu/archives/spr2021/entries/causation-backwards/.

Gasking, D. (1955). Causation and recipes, *Mind*, **64**, 479–87.

Glynn, L. (2013). Causal foundationalism, physical causation, and difference-making, *Synthese*, **190**(6), 1017–37.

Gödel, K. (1949). A remark about the relationship between relativity theory and idealistic philosophy, in P.A. Schilpp, ed., *Albert Einstein: Philosopher-Scientist*, La Salle, IL: Open Court, pp. 557–62.

Greco, J. and Groff, R., eds., (2013). *Powers and Capacities in Philosophy: The New Aristotelianism*, New York: Routledge.

Hausman, D. M. (1982). Causal and explanatory asymmetry, *Proceedings of the Biennial Meeting of the Philosophy of Science Association 1982*, **1**, 43–54.

(1997). Causation, agency, and independence, *Philosophy of Science*, **64** (4 Suppl.), S15–S25.

(1998). *Causal Asymmetries*, Cambridge, UK: Cambridge University Press.

Hitchcock, C. (1996). Causal decision theory and decision-theoretic causation, *Noûs*, **30**(4), 508–26.

(2007). What Russell got right, in H. Price and R. Corry, eds., *Causation, Physics, and the Constitution of Reality*, Oxford: Oxford University Press, pp. 45–65.

Horgan, T. (1981). Counterfactuals and Newcomb's problem, *Journal of Philosophy*, **78**(6), 331–56.

Horwich, P. (1987). *Asymmetries in Time: Problems in the Philosophy of Science*, Cambridge, MA: MIT Press.

Hume, D. [1739–40] (2000). *A Treatise of Human Nature*, D. F. Norton and M. J. Norton, eds., Oxford: Oxford University Press.

Ismael, J. (2007). Freedom, compulsion and causation, *Psyche*, **13**(1), 1–11.

(2012). Decision and the open future, in A. Bardon, ed., *The Future of the Philosophy of Time*, London: Routledge, pp. 149–68.

(2013). Causation, free will, and naturalism, in J. Ladyman and D. Ross, eds., *Scientific Metaphysics*, Oxford: Oxford University Press, pp. 208–35.

(2016). How do causes depend on us? The many faces of perspectivalism, *Synthese*, **193**(1), 245–67.

Jackson, F. and Pargetter, R. (1983). Where the Tickle defence goes wrong, *Australasian Journal of Philosophy*, **61**(3), 295–9.

Jeffrey, R. C. (1981). The logic of decision defended, *Synthese*, **48**, 473–92.

Joyce, J. (2007). Are Newcomb problems really decisions? *Synthese*, **156**(3), 537–62.

Kant, I. [1781/1787] (1996). *The Critique of Pure Reason*, W. S. Pluhar, trans., Indianapolis, IN: Hackett.

Kim, J. (1973). Causation, nomic subsumption, and the concept of event, *Journal of Philosophy*, **70**, 217–36.

Kutach, D. (2002). The entropy theory of counterfactuals, *Philosophy of Science*, **69**(1), 82–104.

(2007). The physical foundations of causation, in H. Price and R. Corry, eds., *Causation, Physics, and the Constitution of Reality*, Oxford: Oxford University Press, pp. 327–50.

(2013). *Causation and Its Basis in Fundamental Physics*, Oxford: Oxford University Press.

Ladyman, J., Ross, D., and Spurrett, D. (2007). Causation in a structural world, in J. Ladyman and D. Ross, eds., *Every Thing Must Go*, Oxford: Oxford University Press, pp. 258–97.

Leeds, S. (2003). Foundations of statistical mechanics – Two approaches, *Philosophy of Science*, **70**(1), 126–44.

Lewis, D. (1973a). Causation, *Journal of Philosophy*, **70**, 556–67 (reprinted in Lewis, 1986).

(1973b). *Counterfactuals*, Oxford: Blackwell.

(1976). The paradoxes of time travel, *American Philosophical Quarterly*, **13** (2), 145–52.

(1979). Counterfactual dependence and time's arrow, *Nous*, **13**, 455–76 (reprinted in Lewis, 1986).

(1981a). Causal decision theory, *Australasian Journal of Philosophy*, **59**(1), 5–30.

(1981b). Are we free to break the laws? *Theoria: A Swedish Journal of Philosophy*, **47**, 113–21.

(1986). *Philosophical Papers*, Vol. II, New York: Oxford University Press.

Loew, C. (2017). The asymmetry of counterfactual dependence, *Philosophy of Science*, **84**(3), 436–55.

Loewer, B. (2007). Counterfactuals and the second law, in H. Price and R. Corry, eds., *Causation, Physics, and the Constitution of Reality*, Oxford: Oxford University Press, pp. 293–326.

2012. Two accounts of laws and time, *Philosophical Studies*, **160**(1), 115–37.

Lowe, E. J. (2002). *A Survey of Metaphysics*, Oxford: Oxford University Press.

Mackie, J. L. (1974). *The Cement of the Universe: A Study of Causation*, Oxford: Clarendon Press.

Maudlin, T. (2002). *Quantum Non-Locality and Relativity*, 2nd ed., Malden, MA: Blackwell.

(2007). *The Metaphysics within Physics*, Oxford: Oxford University Press.

(2019). *Philosophy of Physics: Quantum Mechanics*, Princeton, NJ: Princeton University Press.

Mellor, D. H. (1998). *Real Time II*, London: Routledge.

Menzies, P. (2007). Causation in context, in H. Price and R. Corry, eds., *Causation, Physics, and the Constitution of Reality*, Oxford: Oxford University Press, pp. 191–223.

Menzies, P. and Price, H. (1993). Causation as a secondary quality, *British Journal for the Philosophy of Science*, **44**, 187–203.

Ney, A. (2009). Physical causation and difference-making, *British Journal for the Philosophy of Science*, **60**(4), 737–64.

North, J. (2008). Two views on time reversal, *Philosophy of Science*, **75**(2), 201–23.

Norton, J. D. (2009). Is there an independent principle of causality in physics? *British Journal for the Philosophy of Science*, **60**(3), 475–86.

Nozick, R. (1969). Newcomb's problem and two principles of choice, in N. Rescher, ed., *Essays in Honour of Carl G. Hempel*, Dordrecht: Reidel, pp. 114–46.

Papineau, D. (1985). Causal asymmetry, *British Journal for the Philosophy of Science*, **36**(3), 273–89.

(1992). Can we reduce causal direction to probabilities? *Proceedings of the Biennial Meeting of the Philosophy of Science Association 1992*, **2**, 238–52.

(2001). Evidentialism reconsidered, *Noûs*, **35**, 239–59.

Pearl, J. (2000). *Causality: Models, Reasoning and Inference*, Cambridge, UK: Cambridge University Press.

Price, H. (1984). The philosophy and physics of affecting the past, *Synthese*, **61**(3), 299–323.

(1986). Against causal decision theory, *Synthese*, **67**(2), 195–212.

(1991). Agency and probabilistic causality, *British Journal for the Philosophy of Science*, **42**, 157–76.

(1992a). Agency and causal asymmetry, *Mind*, **101**(403), 501–20.

(1992b). The direction of causation: Ramsey's ultimate contingency, *Proceedings of the Biennial Meeting of the Philosophy of Science Association 1992*, **2**, 253–67.

(1996). *Time's Arrow and Archimedes' Point: New Directions for the Physics of Time*, Oxford: Oxford University Press.

(2007). Causal perspectivalism, in H. Price and R. Corry, eds., *Causation, Physics, and the Constitution of Reality*, Oxford: Oxford University Press, pp. 250–92.

(2012). Causation, chance and the rational significance of supernatural evidence, *Philosophical Review*, **121**(4), 483–538.

(2017). Causation, intervention and agency – Woodward on Menzies and Price, in H. Beebee, C. Hitchcock, and H. Price, eds., *Making a Difference*, Oxford: Oxford University Press, pp. 73–98.

Price, H. and Weslake, B. (2009). The time-asymmetry of causation, in H. Beebee, C. Hitchcock, and P. Menzies, eds., *The Oxford Handbook of Causation*, Oxford: University Press, pp. 414–43.

Ramsey, F. P. [1929] (1978). General propositions and causality, in D. H. Mellor, ed., *Foundations: Essays in Philosophy, Logic, Mathematics and Economics*, London: Routledge & Kegan Paul, pp. 133–51.

Reichenbach, H. (1956). *The Direction of Time*, Berkeley, CA: University of California Press.

Ross, D. and Spurrett, D. (2007). Notions of cause: Russell's thesis revisited, *British Journal for the Philosophy of Science*, **58**(1), 45–76.

Rovelli, C. (2018). *The Order of Time*, London: Allen Lane.

Russell, B. (1912–13). On the notion of cause, *Proceedings of the Aristotelian Society, New Series*, **13**, 1–26.

Schaffer, J. (2016). The metaphysics of causation, in E. N. Zalta, ed., *The Stanford Encyclopedia of Philosophy*, Fall 2016 Edition, Online Encyclopaedia. https://plato.stanford.edu/archives/fall2016/entries/caus ation-metaphysics/.

Sklar, L. (1993). *Physics and Chance*, Cambridge, UK: Cambridge University Press.

Skyrms, B. (1980). *Causal Necessity*, New Haven, CT: Yale University.

Smith, S. R. (2000). Resolving Russell's anti-realism about causation: The connection between causation and the functional dependencies of mathematical physics, *The Monist*, **83**(2), 274–95.

Sobel, J. H. (1994). *Taking Chances: Essays on Rational Choice*, Cambridge, UK: Cambridge University Press.

Sober, E. (1988). The principle of the common cause, in J. H. Fetzer, ed., *Probability and Causality: Essays in Honor of Wesley C. Salmon*, Dordrecht: Springer Netherlands, pp. 211–28.

Sober, E. and Barrett, M. (1992). Conjunctive forks and temporally asymmetric inference, *Australasian Journal of Philosophy*, **70**(1), 1–23.

Spirtes, P., Glymour, C., and Scheines, R. (1993). *Causation, Prediction and Search*, New York: Springer-Verlag.

Strevens, M. (2007a). Why represent causal relations? in A. Gopnik and L. Schulz, eds., *Causal Learning: Psychology, Philosophy, Computation*, Oxford: Oxford University Press, pp. 245–60.

(2007b). Mackie remixed, in J. K. Campbell, M. O'Rourke, and D. Shier, eds., *Causation and Explanation: Topics in Contemporary Philosophy*, Vol. 4, Cambridge, MA: MIT Press, pp. 93–118.

Suppes, P. (1970). *A Probabilistic Theory of Causality*, Amsterdam: North-Holland Publishing Company.

Tooley, M. (1987). *Causation: A Realist Approach*, Oxford: Clarendon Press.

van Fraassen, B. C. (1993). Armstrong, Cartwright, and Earman on laws and symmetry, *Philosophy and Phenomenological Research*, **53**(2), 431–44.

Vihvelin, K. (1991). Freedom, causation and counterfactuals, *Philosophical Studies*, **64**, 161–84.

von Wright, G. (1971). *Explanation and Understanding*, Ithaca, NY: Cornell University Press.

Weslake, B. (2006). Review of making things happen, *Australasian Journal of Philosophy*, **84**(1), 136–40.

Woodward, J. (2003). *Making Things Happen: A Theory of Causal Explanation*, Oxford: Oxford University Press.

(2007). Causation with a human face, in H. Price and R. Corry, eds., *Causation, Physics, and the Constitution of Reality*, Oxford: Oxford University Press, pp. 66–105.

(2016). Causation and manipulability, in E. N. Zalta, ed., *The Stanford Encyclopedia of Philosophy*, Winter 2016 Edition, Online Encyclopaedia. http://plato.stanford.edu/archives/win2016/entries/causation-mani.

Acknowledgements

I'm very grateful to David Albert and Barry Loewer for insightful conversations and comments on the manuscript, as well as to two anonymous reviewers.

Cambridge Elements ≡

The Philosophy of Physics

James Owen Weatherall

University of California, Irvine

James Owen Weatherall is Professor of Logic and Philosophy of Science at the University of California, Irvine. He is the author, with Cailin O'Connor, of *The Misinformation Age: How False Beliefs Spread* (Yale, 2019), which was selected as a *New York Times* Editors' Choice and Recommended Reading by *Scientific American*. His previous books were *Void: The Strange Physics of Nothing* (Yale, 2016) and the *New York Times* bestseller *The Physics of Wall Street: A Brief History of Predicting the Unpredictable* (Houghton Mifflin Harcourt, 2013). He has published approximately fifty peer-reviewed research articles in journals in leading physics and philosophy of science journals and has delivered over 100 invited academic talks and public lectures.

About the Series

This Cambridge Elements series provides concise and structured introductions to all the central topics in the philosophy of physics. The Elements in the series are written by distinguished senior scholars and bright junior scholars with relevant expertise, producing balanced, comprehensive coverage of multiple perspectives in the philosophy of physics.

Cambridge Elements $\equiv$

The Philosophy of Physics

Elements in the Series

A full series listing is available at: www.cambridge.org/EPPH

Printed in the United States
by Baker & Taylor Publisher Services